FIRE OF GOD'S LOVE

FIRE OF
GOD'S LOVE

120

REFLECTIONS
ON THE
EUCHARIST

MIKE AQUILINA

PUBLISHED BY ST. ANTHONY MESSENGER PRESS
CINCINNATI, OHIO

Cover and book design by Mark Sullivan
Cover image © istockphoto.com/John Rodriguez

LIBRARY OF CONGRESS CATALOGING-IN-PUBLICATION DATA

Fire of God's love : 120 reflections on the Eucharist / compiled and introduced
by Mike Aquilina.
p. cm.
Includes bibliographical references and index.
ISBN 978-0-86716-923-2 (pbk. : alk. paper)   1. Lord's Supper—Catholic
Church—Meditations. I. Aquilina, Mike.
BX2235.F57 2009
264'.02036—dc22

2009017270

ISBN 978-0-86716-923-2

Published by Servant Books, an imprint of
St. Anthony Messenger Press.
28 W. Liberty St.
Cincinnati, OH 45202
www.ServantBooks.org

Printed in the United States of America.

Printed on acid-free paper.

09 10 11 12 13 5 4 3 2 1

For Scott Hahn,
friend and table companion,
and always standing by
(see Sirach 6:8–10)

Introduction

The Christian mysteries exceed the capacities of human reason. We could never have discerned these truths if God had not revealed them to us. Ordinary language cannot do them justice. They strain even the specialized vocabularies of the sciences, such as philosophy and theology. They trespass far beyond the frontiers of poetry.

How then can we begin to speak of them?

Sciences falter and poetry fails, but love succeeds by grace. The love of Jesus impels the saints to awestruck silence but also to impassioned speech.

It is Jesus whom the saints know in the Eucharist, the sacrament of the altar. There he is present, Body, Blood, soul and divinity. Under the appearance of a small bit of bread, a drop of wine, God abides in his entirety. The finite contains all infinity, drawing us into communion, making us like himself, sharing his divine nature as generously as once he took up our human nature.

That infinite love is the power behind the words of the saints, the words of Catholics ancient and modern that appear in this book. The Eucharist inspired them to extend the range of science and art, to elevate human words beyond their ordinary reach, to raise them to heaven, as the Eucharist raises the Church even now.

The Eucharist empowers Christians to build up new cultures on the ruins of the old ones. The Jewish historian Miri Rubin has demonstrated how the Church's *profound* belief in the real presence inspired the great achievements of the Middle Ages: the development of hospitals and universities, hospices and hostels. As the old Roman "culture of death" crumbled, Christians were able to build a civilization of love.

That civilization may have blossomed in the Middle Ages, but it was foreseen in the ancient Church. A third-century manual of Church discipline directs, "Widows and orphans are to be revered like the altar."[1] Such a command envisions a social life based on a network of charity, but it presumes a deep eucharistic piety.

The eucharistic kingdom of Christ has arrived, for Jesus reigns in the sacrament. But Saint John Chrysostom urged his fourth-century congregations to hasten the day when that reality was no longer *invisible* but abundantly evident everywhere—in city streets and beside rural roadways. Preaching on the Gospel of Matthew, he said,

> Do you wish to honour the body of Christ? Do not ignore him when he is naked. Do not pay him homage in the temple clad in silk only then to neglect him outside where he suffers cold and nakedness. He who said: "This is my body" is the same One who said: "You saw

me hungry and you gave me no food", and "Whatever you did to the least of my brothers you did also to me"... What good is it if the Eucharistic table is overloaded with golden chalices, when he is dying of hunger? Start by satisfying his hunger, and then with what is left you may adorn the altar as well.[2]

Through the Eucharist God changes us as surely as he changed the elements of bread and wine into himself. He forms us as living stones in the temple of his Church. He builds up a eucharistic culture to replace the culture of death.

Think globally? Act eucharistically. It's the sacrament that renews the earth.

Asking what you can do for your country? Make a good Communion. Make a visit to the tabernacle. Much more will follow.

God will make limitless poetry out of the prose of your life, and he will renew the face of the earth, beginning with your little corner.

The Quotes

1 | *The Spiritual Shortcut*
Holy Communion is the shortest and surest way to Heaven. There are others, innocence, for instance, but that is for little children; penance, but we are afraid of it; generous endurance of the trials of life, but when they come we weep and ask to be spared. Once and for all, beloved children, the surest, easiest, shortest way is by the Eucharist. It is so easy to approach the holy table, and there we taste the joys of Paradise.

—*Pope Saint Pius X*

2 | *The Greatest Work by Far*
Put all the good works in the world against one communion well made, and they are like a speck of dust beside a mountain.

—*Saint John Vianney*

3 | *Letter From a Saint*

I was overjoyed to hear that you are going to experience the precious joy of receiving First Communion on the ninth of June. My dear little brother, it goes without saying that from this moment on, your heart, your spirit and your soul should be occupied with one thought alone: preparing your heart to be God's dwelling place. Oh, yes! Our good Savior must continually be present in your thoughts and you must pray to him to prepare his dwelling place himself so nothing is lacking when he arrives. The angels envy your happiness already, they who possess this God three times holy. They sing his praises without ceasing, but they cannot receive him as we do. How good Jesus is to humble himself to give himself to us and to make of our poor hearts his dwelling place. Invoke the Most Holy Virgin, my dear little friend. Ask her to grant you all the graces you need for this great act.

—Saint Bernadette Soubirous

4 | *The Real Wonder*

The Host that is raised up is the Body of the Living Christ. The Chalice that is lifted up contains His Blood.

This Mystery has sometimes been accompanied by visible miracles, seen not only by holy persons, who were assisting at Mass with great faith; but even by people of little fervour, or by absolute unbelievers.

Once a holy hermit saw the Child Jesus in the Host, and the vision at the Elevation radiated a marvellous light. Once, too, it happened that a rather awkward priest upset the chalice, in which the wine was already consecrated, and spilled it on the altar cloth. The wine, which was white, left red stains like blood, and although the cloth was washed and washed over again the stains could not be removed.

The story is also told of Wittikind, the fierce King of the Saxons, who was converted to Christianity because he saw in the Host at the Elevation the face of a little boy smiling at him....

But the real wonder is worked sacramentally by Christ's coming into the hearts of Christians. The greatest wonder of all is what takes place at every Mass: the real presence of Jesus, hidden from our eyes, but truly present to our faith.

Jesus remains, thus hidden under the appearance of the Sacrament, which is kept in the locked Tabernacle. So every time a Catholic enters his church he bows down devoutly before Him.

The church is a holy place because of this Real Presence of Jesus.

—*Maria Montessori*

5 | *Feeding the Masses*

The only cure for sagging [or] fainting faith is Communion. Though always Itself, perfect and complete and inviolate, the Blessed Sacrament does not operate completely and once for all in any of us. Like the act of Faith it must be continuous and grow by exercise. Frequency is of the highest effect. Seven times a week is more nourishing than seven times at intervals. Also I can recommend this as an exercise (alas! only too easy to find opportunity for): make your communion in circumstances that affront your taste. Choose a snuffling or gabbling priest or a proud and vulgar friar; and a church full of the usual bourgeois crowd, ill-behaved children—from those who yell to those products of Catholic schools who the moment the tabernacle is opened sit back and yawn— open necked and dirty youths, women in trousers and often with hair both unkempt and uncovered. Go to Communion *with* them (and pray for them). It will be just the same (or better than that) as a mass said beautifully by a visibly holy man, and shared by a few devout and decorous people. (It could not be worse than the mess of the feeding of the Five Thousand—after which [Our] Lord propounded the feeding that was to come.)

—*J.R.R. Tolkien*

6 | *Calming the Storms*

What does Jesus intend this total gift of Himself will bring? Peace, transformation, and unification both now and (unconditionally) in the kingdom to come. I can attest to the remarkable efficacy of all three of these graces in my own life. With respect to peace, I can remember going to Mass with very disturbing thoughts in my mind (having received bad news, or having been criticized or irritated by someone's actions, etc.). I carried the "tape playing" and emotional discharge associated with those things right into the Mass with me—which sometimes provoked an intensification of internal disturbance during the Mass. But many, many have been the times when a deep calm (beyond myself) replaced the disturbance as I approached and received the Holy Eucharist. I have difficulty attributing this change of condition to mere self-delusion, because wishful thinking has never overcome "intense disturbance" in any other circumstance in my life. Why the Holy Eucharist? Why so frequently? Hmm....

—*Robert Spitzer, S.J.*

7 | *Everyday Graces*

When you think of going to Mass on working days, it is an impulse of the grace that God wills to grant you. Follow it.

—*Saint John Vianney*

8 | *Saving Time*

The best way to economize time is to "lose" half an hour each day attending Holy Mass.

—*Blessed Frederic Ozanam*

9 | *Satisfaction*

Never neglect to satiate yourself with the food of the angels.

—*Saint Pio of Pietrelcina*

10 | *Our Daily Bread*

"Give us this day our daily bread."

When the words of Christ have been uttered, it is no longer called bread, but is named "body." Why then, in the Lord's Prayer, does He say "bread"?

Indeed, He did call it bread, but He called it *epiousion,* which is Greek for "supersubstantial." So it is not bread that passes into the body. It is, rather, the "bread of eternal life" (see Jn 6:35–58), which supports the substance of our soul.

The Latin, however, calls this bread "daily." But if it is "daily" bread, then why do you take it so infrequently? Take daily what will help you daily. And live so that you deserve to receive it daily. He who does not deserve to receive it daily, does not deserve to receive it once a year. Holy Job offered sacrifice daily for his sons, just in case they had sinned in heart or word (see Jb 1:5).

As often as the sacrifice is offered, the Lord's death, the Lord's resurrection, the Lord's ascension, and the remission of sins are signified—and still you don't take this bread of life daily? He who has a wound needs a medicine. The wound is that we are under sin; the medicine is the heavenly and venerable sacrament.

Give us this day our daily bread. If you receive daily, daily is today for you.

—*Saint Ambrose of Milan*

11 | *Doing Business*

In over forty years I had never, without good reason, missed a Sunday Mass. Now I started every single day on my knees in church. To me there is nothing shameful about praying when you're in trouble. If prayer has been the habit of a lifetime it's the natural thing to do. If you have never prayed before it's a good time to start. Either way there can be times when you are overwhelmed and there is no place else to turn.

Such times now came to me. And each time the walls were about to close in and crush me, when there was no light for even one step ahead, "something" happened—a bellboy thrust his life savings into my hand, a difficult business rival took everything I had with one hand and gave it back with the other, a promise that meant my business life was broken by one man and seven others stepped in to fill the breach.

Could I take credit for personal cleverness in things like that? I could not. To me they were answered prayer.

—*Conrad Hilton*

12 | *The Sound of Silence*

The Canon of the Mass guides us silently to the heart of the Mystery. In silence we go to meet Silence. We wait "until He come". Our eyes, we know, will not see Him, our hands will not touch Him. God is a Spirit; He remains such even in the Sacred Humanity which gives Him to us.

God is a Secret audible only when self is silent.

—*Maurice Zundel*

13 | *Universal Devotion*

And yet there is this: the attentive reverence of Catholics at the eucharistic prayer, and most notably at the consecration and elevation of the elements. At least that is, with notable exceptions, my experience. It is so intense that you can, so to speak, cut it with a knife.... [T]here is this almost electric intensity of devotion toward what God is doing, toward the reality that Christ is keeping his promise once again when we "do this" in remembrance of him. Or so I have found it to be in parishes around the country, in corrugated huts in the slums of Mexico City, in the basilicas of Rome, in a bombed-out schoolhouse in Nigeria, in a Polish priory, in a village church of northern Quebec.... It is quiet, undemonstratively earnest, a palpable yearning for a gift desired, a sigh of gratitude for a gift received. "It" is happening again. It is the Mass that holds together the maddeningly ragtag and variegated thing that is the Catholic Church.

—*Richard John Neuhaus*

14 | *Reasons to Believe*

Clearly I had good reasons for believing.... I could see that *everyone*—my parents, my big brothers and sisters, all the strange crowds that filled out church on Sunday—had known the wonderful secret I had learned, and believed it too. Anyone could see how sure they were, especially when the Eucharist was held up before them at the altar. Most of them were saying quietly, "My Lord and my God," the very words my mother told me to say.

For it made sense of so much. If God made us, and all things, he had to stick with us in this wonderful and dangerous world. Of course, like all little boys, I loved this strange world. But already I had learned how fragile it is: when our dog died; when I got a bad ear ache and could not understand it; when a greatuncle died. In this puzzling world, we all needed to know just where the Lord is. God is everywhere, but Jesus, God who became our brother, and bears divinity with human approachability, is right here....

Now that I am a priest, and say Mass for crowds of people, I see how calm and deep is the faith of the great numbers who crowd into church every Sunday.

When I raise the host that has become the body of Jesus our Savior, I realize that they are adoring him as willingly as I do. When I raise the chalice that holds his precious blood, which was shed to save the whole world from all its most bitter sorrows, their faith supports my own. Then it is a great joy to cry out: "Let us proclaim the mystery of faith!" This faith is not a burden: it lifts us up.

—*Ronald Lawler*, O.F.M. CAP.

15 | *The Look of Love*

[T]o participate in the Mass here and now is not a matter of looking down or looking around, but of looking up—it's a taste of what awaits us, through the grace and mercy of God, for all eternity. True worship, like true love, doesn't mean looking into each other's eyes; it means looking together, in love, at the One who is Love all the way through.

—*George Weigel*

16 | *The Son Is the Sun*

What the sun in the heavens is to all nature, shedding light and imparting warmth, the Eucharistic Sacrifice is in the house of God, beautifying and adorning its every feast with celestial splendor.

—*Nicholas Gihr*

17 | *Where Are We?*

We knew not whether we were in heaven or on earth. For on earth there is no such splendor or such beauty, and we are at a loss how to describe it. We know only that God dwells there among men, and their service is fairer than the ceremonies of other nations. For we cannot forget that beauty.

—*Emissaries of Prince Vladimir of Kiev, AD 988,*
describing the Christian liturgy in Constantinople

18 | *A Matter of Love*

"The Mass is long," you say, and I reply: "Because your love is short."

—*Saint Josemaría Escrivá*

19 | *What's Happening Now*

As often as you celebrate or hear Mass, it should seem as great, as new, as sweet to you as if on that very day Christ became man in the womb of the Virgin, or, hanging on the Cross, suffered and died for the salvation of man.

—*Thomas à Kempis*

20 | *Mighty Rites*

[I]t is fitting that the Divine Majesty manifests Its power most fully in these blessed rites, and because as long as a person remains within these things that belong to God, God's will never leaves him.

—*Blessed Hildegard of Bingen*

21 | *Ascension Homily: Angels at Mass*

The angels are present here. The angels and the martyrs meet today. If you wish to see the angels and the martyrs, open the eyes of faith and look upon this sight. For if the very air is filled with angels, how much more so the Church! And if the Church is filled with angels, how much more is that true today when their Lord has risen into heaven! The whole air about us is filled with angels.

—*Saint John Chrysostom*

22 | *Here for You*

When our Lord instituted the Eucharist during the Last Supper, night had already fallen. The world had fallen into darkness, for the old rites, the old signs of God's infinite mercy to mankind, were going to be brought to fulfilment. The way was opening to a new dawn—the new Passover. The Eucharist was instituted during that night, preparing in advance for the morning of the Resurrection.

Jesus has remained in the Eucharist for love...for you.

—He has remained, knowing how men would treat him...and how you would treat him.

—He has remained so that you could eat him, and visit him and tell him your concerns; and so that, by your prayer beside the tabernacle and by receiving him sacramentally, you could fall more in love each day, and help other souls, many souls, to follow the same path.

Good child: see how lovers on earth kiss the flowers, the letters, the mementos of those they love....

Then you, how could you ever forget that you have him always at your side—yes, *Him*? How could you forget...that you can eat him?

—Lord, may I never again flutter along close to the ground. Illumined by the rays of the divine Sun—Christ—in the Eucharist, may my flight never be interrupted until I find repose in your Heart.

—*Saint Josemaría Escrivá*

23 | *We Cannot Live Without the Mass*

"These persons, being Christians, have held an assembly for the Mass, contrary to the edict of the Emperors Diocletian and Maximian." So read the charges brought against a congregation in Abitina in North Africa, in AD 304.

"What is your rank?" asked the proconsul Anulinus of the first prisoner brought to him.

"I am a senator," replied Dativus.

"Were you there in the assembly?"

"I am a Christian and I was there in the assembly."

Immediately the proconsul ordered him to be suspended on the rack and his body torn by barbed hooks....

Then Saturninus, the priest, was called forward for combat.

The proconsul asked, "Did you, contrary to the orders of the emperors, arrange for these persons to hold an assembly?"

Saturninus replied, "Certainly. We celebrated the Mass."

"Why?"

"Because we cannot live without the Mass."

As soon as he said this, the proconsul ordered him to be put immediately on the rack with Dativus....

Then Felix, a son of Saturninus and a lector in the Church, came forward to the contest. And the proconsul asked him,... "Were you one of the assembly...?"

"As if a Christian could exist without the Mass, or the Mass exist without a Christian!" answered Felix. "Don't you know that Christians make the Mass, and the Mass makes Christians? Neither can exist without the other. We celebrated our assembly gloriously."

—Acts of the Martyrs of Abitina

24 | *Taking Part in the Mass*

To offer oneself up with Christ; to immolate oneself with him, does that mean we are to go up to Calvary and shed our blood? No, certainly. It means that we should take part in the Mass, in an intelligent and active way, that we should try to understand what the priest is doing, express our union with him and among ourselves by our answers, our singing, our postures. It means above all that we should not content ourselves with going to Mass as a ceremony that has no influence on our lives but that there we resolve, and there we draw strength, to destroy all that is opposed to our union with God, and to develop all that deepens that union, that is to say first and above all, charity, our devotedness to God and our fellow men. The Mass, the Eucharist, is the sacrament of sacrifice which means, finally, of our deification by the generous gift of ourselves.

—*A.M. Roguet, O.P.*

25 | *Words of a Martyr*

Let me become food for the wild beasts, through whom I can attain to God. I am God's wheat. Let me be ground by the teeth of the wild beasts, that I may be found the pure bread of Christ. Rather entice the wild beasts, that they may become my tomb, and may leave nothing of my body; so that when I have fallen asleep [in death], I may be no trouble to any one. Then shall I truly be a disciple of Christ, when the world shall not see so much as my body....

...For though I am alive while I write to you, yet I am eager to die. My love has been crucified, and there is no fire in me desiring to be fed; but there is within me a water that lives and speaks, saying to me inwardly, "Come to the Father." I have no delight in corruptible food, nor in the pleasures of this life. I desire the bread of God, the heavenly bread, the bread of life, which is the flesh of Jesus Christ, the Son of God, who became afterward of the seed of David and Abraham; and I desire the drink of God, namely his blood, which is incorruptible love and eternal life.

—*Saint Ignatius of Antioch*

26 | *Transform Me*

Among the grains of purest wheat,
   O happy lot! he chooses me.
   We lose our life for Him, the Christ —
   What rapturous height of ecstasy!
   Thy spouse am I, Thy chosen one.
   My Well-Beloved! come, dwell in me.
   Thy beauty wins my heart. Oh, come!
   Deign to transform me into Thee!

—*Saint Thérèse of Lisieux*

27 | *The Host's Beating Heart*

Every time I hear anyone speak of the Sacred Heart of Jesus or of the Blessed Sacrament I feel an indescribable joy. It is as if a wave of precious memories, sweet affections and joyful hopes swept over my poor person, making me tremble with happiness and filling my soul with tenderness. These are loving appeals from Jesus who wants me whole-heartedly there, at the source of all goodness, his Sacred Heart, throbbing mysteriously behind the Eucharistic veils. The devotion to the Sacred Heart has grown with me all my life.

—Angelo Roncalli (later Pope John XXIII)

28 | *A Foreshadowing*

[T]he offering of fine flour, prescribed [in the Old Testament] to be presented on behalf of those purified from leprosy, was a foreshadowing of the bread of the Eucharist. This celebration Our Lord Jesus Christ prescribed in remembrance of the suffering he endured on behalf of those who are purified in soul from all iniquity.

—Saint Justin Martyr

29 | *The Infinite Banquet*

The bread that the firstborn broke in the desert
was very good, but consumed and passed away.
He returned again and broke the New Bread,
which ages and generations shall not exhaust.

He broke seven loaves that also ran out,
and the five loaves he multiplied were consumed.
Yet the one bread he broke exceeded the world's needs,
for as it was divided, it was multiplied more.

With much wine, too, he filled the stone jars;
they drew it out abundantly, and yet it failed.
Yet the cup that he gave, though the draught was small,
was great in its strength, with no end to its power.

—*Saint Ephrem of Syria*

30 | *Answer Me*

Q. 871. *What do we mean when we say the Sacrament which contains the Body and Blood?*

A. When we say the Sacrament which contains the Body and Blood, we mean the Sacrament which is the Body and Blood, for after the Consecration there is no other substance present in the Eucharist.

Q. 872. *When is the Holy Eucharist a Sacrament, and when is it a sacrifice?*

A. The Holy Eucharist is a Sacrament when we receive it in Holy Communion and when it remains in the Tabernacle of the Altar. It is a sacrifice when it is offered up at Mass by the separate Consecration of the bread and wine, which signifies the separation of Our Lord's blood from His body when He died on the Cross.

Q. 873. *When did Christ institute the Holy Eucharist?*

A. Christ instituted the Holy Eucharist at the Last Supper, the night before He died.

. . .

Q. 880. *How do we show that Christ did change bread and wine into the substance of His body and blood?*

A. We show that Christ did change bread and wine into the substance of His body and blood:

1. From the words by which He promised the Holy Eucharist;
2. From the words by which He instituted the Holy Eucharist;
3. From the constant use of the Holy Eucharist in the Church since the time of the Apostles;
4. From the impossibility of denying the Real Presence in the Holy Eucharist, without likewise denying all that Christ has taught and done; for we have stronger proofs for the Holy Eucharist than for any other Christian truth.

—Baltimore Catechism

31 | *Things Seen and Unseen*

The human soul, which is *invisible, invisibly* receives the sacrament, which exists *invisibly* in that oblation, while the human body, which is *visible, visibly* receives the oblation that visibly embodies that sacrament.

—Blessed Hildegard of Bingen

32 | *The Climax of History*

When the priest says the words of consecration, he pauses in wonder at this *mysterium fidei* [mystery of faith]. For it is doubly a mystery—the mystery of Christ's unfathomable sacrifice, and the mystery of that sacrifice made present to us. Between the sacrifice of Calvary and the sacrifice of the altar the only difference is in the way it is present. The Mass is the one and only Tree of the Cross planted in our midst that we may eat its fruits.

A *mysterium tremendum,* said the early Christians, a fearful mystery. They were right. Christ is present to us in the most majestic moment of history, the moment of his sacrifice in which the world of sin dies, and the world of the last days is created in God's love. We sing, "Holy, Holy, Holy!" not only to acclaim the Lord coming in glory, but to adore the Godhead entering our lives at that moment.

A fearful mystery of faith, but a mystery of joy too. It is what gives the Church her exultant joy and her hope; it is her one treasure. Christ at the moment of the Redemption is in her midst, and with him all the riches of that redemption. We need only faith to believe.

—*François Xavier Durrwell*

33 | *Sing the Savior's Glory*

On the night of that Last Supper
Seated with His chosen band,
He the Paschal victim eating,
First fulfills the Law's command;
Then as Food to His Apostles
Gives Himself with His own hand.

Word-made-flesh, the bread of nature
By His word to Flesh He turns;
wine into His Blood He changes;
what though sense no change discerns?
Only be the heart in earnest,
faith her lesson quickly learns.

Down in adoration falling,
Lo! the sacred Host we hail;
Lo! o'er ancient forms departing,
newer rites of grace prevail;
faith for all defects supplying,
where the feeble senses fail.

—*Saint Thomas Aquinas*

34 | *What Children Can Know*

It is easiest to tell what transubstantiation is by saying this: little children should be taught about it as early as possible. Not of course using the word "transubstantiation," because it is not a little child's word. But the thing can be taught, and it is best taught at mass at the consecration.... "Look! Look what the priest is doing.... He is saying Jesus' words that change the bread into Jesus' body. Now he's lifting it up. Look! Now bow your head and say 'My Lord and my God.'" ...This need not be disturbing to the surrounding people....

...The little child can grasp this and it is implicit in the act of worship that follows the teaching. I knew a child, close upon three years old and only then beginning to talk, but taught as I have described, who was in the free space at the back of the church when the mother went to communion. "Is he in you?" the child asked when the mother came back. "Yes," she said, and to her amazement the child prostrated itself before her. I can testify to this, for I saw it happen.

—*G.E.M. Anscombe*

35 | *Mary's Milk, the Body of Christ*

God so loved the world that He gave His only begotten Son. And that Son loved God and us, His brothers, so that He lay on the altar of the Cross and sacrificed His life for us in worship and atonement.

He was our life gaining for us eternal life. Showing us the way of love and surrender, suffering and death. So He must also be our food, our bread and wine, our meat indeed. This is literally true.

The flesh of Jesus is the flesh of Mary, St. Augustine says. He is man as we are with all our strivings, labors, fatigues, temptations. When we take Him, His life, His flesh and blood, we become Him.

We drink our mother's milk from her body. Her blood nourishes us as we lie in her womb. Mary's blood nourishes Christ, and His blood nourishes us. He drank from her body and became man. We eat His body and drink His blood and become God. It is reasonable for us to believe this but we cannot understand it.

—*Dorothy Day*

36 | *Plain Speaking*

"This is my body," "this is my blood"; under no circumstance may the *is* in these holiest of sentences be interpreted as "means" or "is a symbol of" my body and blood. If ever the Lord's admonition, "Let your speech be, 'Yes, yes'; 'No, no'; and whatever is beyond these comes from the evil one" [Matthew 5:37] was deeply urgent, it is here.

It is not only wrong but sacrilegious to tamper with these words. What they express is simplest truth, and what takes place pure reality. He who speaks is neither a *great* nor *the greatest* religious personality of the millennia, but the Son of God.

His words are no expression of mystical profundity, but a command of Him who has all earthly and heavenly power. They have no equivalent in human speech, for they are words of Omnipotence. We can compare them only with other words of the Lord, when "He arose and rebuked the wind and the sea, and there came a great calm" [Matthew 8:26]; or, to the leper: "I will, be thou made clean" [Matthew 8:3]; or to Jairus' dead child, "Girl, arise!" [Luke 8:54] Their real equivalent is the Father's "Be!" (light made) from which creation itself emerged. [Genesis 1:3]

—*Romano Guardini*

37 | *The Unavoidable Truth*

He who eats my flesh and drinks my blood has eternal life, and I will raise him up at the last day. For my flesh is food indeed, and my blood is drink indeed.—John 6:54–55

Could Christ have meant those words literally? It is hard to take them that way. The people to whom Jesus addressed those words "murmured" and "strove among themselves" and called it a "hard saying." Jesus knew this, knew that even his disciples were offended by such talk.

Could anyone be more scandalized at the notion of drinking blood than a good Jew? Jesus was a born Jew. His disciples ate kosher food, kept Passover, and had a holy horror of consuming blood, which was the symbol of life, set apart by the Law, and used only in sacrifice and worship of the true God. The Christ would not speak idly or carelessly, or in unexplained metaphor, when he spoke of his own blood. He could have watered down what he said. He could have said he spoke in a parable, that he didn't really mean people were to eat him. But he wouldn't do that. He watched hundreds of hitherto ardent followers turn their backs on him and go away rather than believe what sounded like repulsive nonsense. He let them go. Because what he said was true, and couldn't be explained away to accommodate those who were scandalized.

When I got that into my head, I couldn't sleep. In the darkness, while the steam heat of the apartment radiator died away and the night sounds of the city came in through a sooty window, I lay pondering the fact that only in one Church and its Orthodox sister was there still being offered the real flesh and blood of the Christ.

—*April Oursler Armstrong*

38 | *How Can He Do This?*

If the Word of God is living and active (Hebrews 4:12), and the Lord did all that he willed; if he said, "Let there be light," and there was light, "Let there be a firmament," and there was a firmament; if the heavens were established by the Word of the Lord and all the host of them by the breath of his mouth; ...if God the Word of his own will became man and the pure and undefiled blood of the Holy Ever-Virgin made his flesh without the help of seed—can he not then make the bread his body and the wine and water his blood? He said in the beginning, "Let the earth bring forth grass" (Genesis 1:11), and even to this present day, when the rain comes it brings forth its proper fruits, urged on and strengthened by the divine command. God said, "This is my body," and, "This is my blood," and, "Do this in remembrance of me." And so it is at his omnipotent command until he come again.

—*Saint John of Damascus*

39 | *Your Privileges*

What is in the chalice is the same as what flowed from the side of Christ, and of this we are made partakers....

...What the Lord did not tolerate on the cross [the breaking of his limbs], he tolerates now in the sacrifice, for the love of you; he lets himself be broken into pieces, so that he may fill all men....

...The wise men adored this body when it lay in the manger;...they prostrated themselves before it in fear and trembling.... Now you behold the same body that the wise men adored in the manger, lying upon the altar;...you also know its power and salutary effect....

...Already, in the present life, this mystery changes the earth for you into heaven.... The most sublime thing that is there, the body of the Lord,...you can behold here on earth.... And you not only behold it, but you touch it and consume it.

—*Saint John Chrysostom*

40 | *The Power of the Word*

Thou sayest perhaps, "My bread is of the usual kind." But that bread is bread before the words of the sacraments; when consecration has been added, from bread it becomes the flesh of Christ. Let us therefore prove this. How can that which is bread be the body of Christ? By consecration. But in what words and in whose language is the consecration? Those of the Lord Jesus. For all the other things which are said in the earlier parts of the service are said by the priest—praises are offered to God, prayer is asked for the people, for kings, and the rest; when it comes to the consecration of the venerable sacrament, the priest no longer uses his own language, but he uses the language of Christ. Therefore, the word of Christ consecrates this sacrament.

What is the word of Christ? That, to be sure, whereby all things are made. The Lord commanded, and the heaven was made; the Lord commanded, and the earth was made; the Lord commanded, and the seas were made; the Lord commanded, and every creature was produced. Thou seest, therefore, how effective is the word of Christ. If, therefore, there is such power in the word of the Lord Jesus, that the things which were not began to be, how much more is it effective, that things previously existing should, without ceasing to exist, be changed into something else? The heaven was not, the sea was not, the earth was not; but hear David saying, *He spake, and they were made: he commanded, and they were created.*

Therefore, that I may answer thee, it was not the body of Christ before consecration; but after consecration, I tell thee, it is now the body of Christ. *He spake, and* it was made: *he commanded, and* it was created. Thou thyself didst formerly exist, but thou wast an old creature; after thou wast consecrated, thou didst begin to be a new creature.

—Saint Ambrose of Milan

41 | *The Mass in AD 155*

On the day we call the day of the sun, all who dwell in the city or country gather in the same place.

The memoirs of the apostles and the writings of the prophets are read, as much as time permits.

When the reader has finished, he who presides over those gathered admonishes and challenges them to imitate these beautiful things.

Then we all rise together and offer prayers for ourselves . . . and for all others, wherever they may be, so that we may be found righteous by our life and actions, and faithful to the commandments, so as to obtain eternal salvation.

When the prayers are concluded we exchange the kiss.

Then someone brings bread and a cup of water and wine mixed together to him who presides over the brethren.

He takes them and offers praise and glory to the Father of the universe, through the name of the Son and of the Holy Spirit and for a considerable time he gives thanks (in Greek: *eucharistian*) that we have been judged worthy of these gifts.

When he has concluded the prayers and thanksgivings, all present give voice to an acclamation by saying: "Amen."

When he who presides has given thanks and the people have responded, those whom we call deacons give to those present the "eucharisted" bread, wine and water and take them to those who are absent.

—*Saint Justin Martyr*

42 | *Heaven's Mysteries*

The Son's mysteries are fire among the heavenly beings;
Isaiah bears witness with us to having seen them. The
mysteries which were in the Divinity's bosom are distrib-
uted to Adam's children on the altar. The altar is fashioned
like the cherubim's chariot and is surrounded by the
heavenly hosts; on the altar is laid the Body of God's Son,
and Adam's children carry it solemnly in their hands.

—Saint James of Sarugh

43 | *Spirit and Fire*

In your bread is hidden the Spirit that cannot be eaten.
In your wine dwells the fire that cannot be drunk.
Your Spirit in the bread and the fire in your cup
are true miracles, which our lips receive.

When the Lord came down to earth, to mortal men,
he made of them a new creation.
As in the angels he mingled fire and spirit,
that they might be of fire and spirit in a hidden way.

The seraph did not bring the living coal near with his
    fingers.
It did not come close to Isaiah's mouth.
He did not himself lay hold of it or eat it.
But to us the Lord has given them both.

To the angelic spirits Abraham brought food, and they
    ate.
Now comes a new miracle, that our mighty Lord
gives bodily creatures both fire and Spirit as food and
    drink....

As fire came down on the sacrifice of Elijah and
    consumed it,
the fire of mercy has become for us a living sacrifice.
Fire ate up the offerings, and we, O Lord, have eaten
    your fire in your offering....
In the bread and the cup is fire and the Holy Spirit.

—*Saint Ephrem of Syria*

44 | *If Only...*

How many nowadays say, "If only I could gaze upon his form, his figure, his clothing, his shoes!" Behold, you do see him, touch him, eat him!... He gives himself to you, not merely to look upon, but even to touch, to eat, and to receive within you....

...Think about the table where you are eating, and whose it is! For we are fed with something angels view with awe, something they cannot contemplate without fear because of its splendor. We become one mass with him; we become one body and one flesh with Christ.... What shepherd feeds his sheep with his own flesh? ...Some mothers... entrust their newborn infants to wet nurses; but this he did not wish to do. Instead he nourishes us with his own Blood, he unites himself with us.

...These are not deeds of human power....We take the place of servants; it is he who consecrates and changes [the bread and wine].

—*Saint John Chrysostom*

45 | *Nearer, My God, to Thee*

Lord Jesus, you are in the Holy Eucharist. You are there, a yard away in the tabernacle. Your body, your soul, your human nature, your divinity, your whole being is there, in its twofold nature. How close you are, my God, my Savior, my Jesus, my Brother, my Spouse, my Beloved!

You were not nearer to the Blessed Virgin during the nine months she carried you in her womb than you are to me when you rest on my tongue at Holy Communion. You were no closer to the Blessed Virgin and St. Joseph in the caves at Bethlehem or the house at Nazareth or during the flight into Egypt, or at any moment of that divine family life than you are to me at this moment—and so many others—in the tabernacle. St. Mary Magdalene was no closer to you when she sat at your feet at Bethany than I am here at the foot of this altar. You were no nearer to your apostles when you were sitting in the midst of them than you are to me now, my God. How blessed I am!

—*Blessed Charles de Foucauld*

46 | *Credo!*

Amen, amen, amen. I believe, I believe, I believe and confess to the last breath that this is the Life-giving Flesh, that of the Only-begotten Son, our Lord and our God, our Savior Jesus Christ.

—*Ancient Egyptian Eucharistic Prayer*

47 | *Be Not Afraid*

O my brethren, here is mystery without mitigation, without relief!…that now, under the form of Bread, He should lie upon our Altars, and suffer Himself to be hidden in a small tabernacle!

Most incomprehensible, but still, while the thought overwhelms our imagination, it also overpowers our heart; it is the most subduing, affecting, piercing thought which can be pictured to us. It thrills through us, and draws our tears, and abases us, and melts us into love and affection, when we dwell upon it. O most tender and compassionate Lord! You see, He puts out of our sight that mysteriousness of His, which is only awful and terrible; He insists not on His past eternity; He would not scare and trouble His poor children, when at length He speaks to them; no, He does but surround Himself with His own infinite bountifulness and compassion; He bids His Church tell us only of His mysterious condescension.

—*Venerable John Henry Newman*

48 | *The Unimaginable*

What man could not have imagined, God has done. What man could not utter, nor conceive, and what he could never have desired—that, God in his love has uttered, conceived, and executed. Should we ever have dared to suggest to God that he should make his Son die for us, that he should give us his Flesh to eat and his Blood to drink?

—*Saint John Vianney*

49 | *Be What You See*

If you are Christ's body and members, it is your mystery that is placed on the table of the Lord, it is your mystery that you receive…. Be what you see and receive what you are.

—*Saint Augustine*

50 | *Picture This*

Exercise your ordinary imagination, picturing the Savior to yourself in his sacred humanity as if he were beside you just as we are wont to think of our friends, and imagine that we see or hear them at our side. But when the Blessed Sacrament of the Altar is there, then this Presence is no longer imaginary, but most real; and the sacred species are but a veil from behind which the present Savior beholds and considers us, although we cannot see him as he is.

—*Saint Francis de Sales*

51 | *Mad With Love*

O boundless charity!
Just as you gave us yourself,
wholly God and wholly man,
so you left us all of yourself as food
so that while we are pilgrims in this life
we might not collapse in our weariness
but be strengthened by you, heavenly food.
O mercenary people!
And what has your God left you?
He has left you himself,

wholly God and wholly man,

hidden under the whiteness of this bread.

O fire of love!

Was it not enough to gift us

with creation in your image and likeness,

and to create us anew to grace in your Son's blood,

without giving us yourself as food,

the whole of divine being,

the whole of God?

What drove you?

Nothing but your charity,

mad with love as you are!

—Saint Catherine of Siena

52 | *Models of Devotion*

With what awe and grateful love should we assist at this sacrifice! The angels were present at Calvary. Angels also are present at the Mass. If we cannot assist with the seraphic love and rapt attention of the angelic spirits, let us worship, at least, with the simple devotion of the shepherds of Bethlehem, and the unswerving faith of the Magi. Let us offer to our God the golden gift of a heart full of love, and the incense of our praise and adoration repeating often during the holy oblation the words of the Psalmist: "The mercies of the Lord I will sing forever."

—Cardinal James Gibbons

53 | *Lost in Wonder*

The Lord whom the seraphs fear to look at, the same you behold in Bread and Wine on the altar.

—*Liturgy of Saint James*

54 | *The End Is Here*

The sign of the cross appears upon the eucharistic, sacrificial meal. This is a sign of sorrow and mourning; the lamb of God has been slain. Yet, this divine sorrow does not exclude joy; instead, it gives a foretaste of a glorious banquet of heavenly joys. The Christian pasch is not so much the descent of heaven upon the earth but rather the earthly is lifted up to the heavenly. "For Christ, our passover, has been sacrificed. Therefore, let us keep festival!" The *eschaton* or final day has arrived—at least for a moment. The glorified Christ is in our midst.

The consecration and communion sound the notes of the angels' trumpets, announcing the *parousia* or triumphant presence of Jesus. He who went into a distant country to obtain a kingdom for us has returned. "When Christ your life appears," St. Paul writes, "then you shall appear with him in glory" (Col 3:4). At each Mass, Jesus is summoning his followers, "Come, rise from the dead. This is the day which the Lord has made." Forming one family with all Christians and looking to the risen Christ at the head of the table, all worshippers begin a new, heavenly life with each eucharistic repast.

—*Carroll Stuhlmueller, C.P.*

55 | *Where Are You Now?*

For when you see the Lord sacrificed, and laid upon the altar, and the priest standing and praying over the victim, and all the worshippers empurpled with that precious blood, can you then think that you are still among men, and standing upon the earth? Are you not, on the contrary, immediately transported to heaven?

—Saint John Chrysostom

56 | *Right Intention*

The Holy Eucharist is a great means through which to aspire to perfection. But we must receive it with the desire and intention of removing from the heart all that is displeasing to him with whom we wish to dwell.

—Saint Pio of Pietrelcina

57 | *Take It to Mass*

The supreme and eternal Priest, Christ Jesus, since he wills to continue his witness and service also through the laity, vivifies them in this Spirit and increasingly urges them on to every good and perfect work.

For besides intimately linking them to His life and His mission, He also gives them a sharing in His priestly function of offering spiritual worship for the glory of God and the salvation of men. For this reason the laity, dedicated to Christ and anointed by the Holy Spirit, are marvelously called and wonderfully prepared so that ever more abundant fruits of the Spirit may be produced in them. For all their works, prayers and apostolic endeavors, their ordinary married and family life, their daily occupations, their physical and mental relaxation, if carried out in the Spirit, and even the hardships of life, if patiently borne—all these become "spiritual sacrifices acceptable to God through Jesus Christ" [1 Peter 2:5]. Together with the offering of the Lord's body, they are most fittingly offered in the celebration of the Eucharist. Thus, as those everywhere who adore in holy activity, the laity consecrate the world itself to God.

—*Second Vatican Council*

58 | *The Span of a Mass*

Such is the greatness and the grandeur of the Holy Mass. It leads us in its mysteries up to the very gates of heaven and, at the same time, embraces the humblest duties and hardships of daily life.

—*Matthias Eberhard*

59 | *The Center of Life*

Through the liturgy rightly understood and lived...all our life is centered in Christ and the Christ-life radiates out into every action of the day.

—*Virgil Michel, O.S.B.*

60 | *Heaven on Earth*

Our whole life gets caught up in the Mass and becomes our participation in the Mass. As heaven descends to earth, we lift up our earth to meet it halfway. That's the splendor of the ordinary: the workaday world becomes our Mass. That's how we bring about the Kingdom of God. When we begin to see that heaven awaits us in the Mass, we begin already to bring our home to heaven. And we begin already to bring heaven home with us.

We become martyrs, witnesses to Jesus Christ, Whose *Parousia*, Whose Presence, we know most intimately.

We were made as creatures on earth, but we were made for heaven, and nothing less. We were made in time like Adam and Eve, yet not to remain in an earthly paradise, but to be taken up into the eternal life of God Himself.

Now, heaven has been unveiled for us with the death and resurrection of Jesus Christ. *Now* is the Communion God has created us for. *Now*, heaven touches earth and awaits you. Jesus Christ himself says to you: "Behold, I stand at the door and knock; if anyone hears my voice and opens the door, *I will come in to him and eat with him, and he with me*" (Rev 3:20).

The door opens *now* on the marriage supper of the Lamb.

—*Scott Hahn*

61 | *Where Love Leads*

The more ardent the love for the Eucharist in the hearts of the Christian people, the more clearly will they recognize the goal of all mission: *to bring Christ to others.* Not just a theory or a way of life inspired by Christ, but the gift of his very person. Anyone who has not shared the truth of love with his brothers and sisters has not yet given enough.

—*Pope Benedict XVI*

62 | *The Name and Face of Happiness*

[T]he happiness you have a right to enjoy has a name and a face: it is Jesus of Nazareth, hidden in the Eucharist. Only he gives the fullness of life to humanity! With Mary, say your own "yes" to God, for he wishes to give himself to you.

—*Pope Benedict XVI*

63 | *The Tasks of the Day*

The duties and cares of the day ahead crowd about us when we awake in the morning (if they have not already dispelled our night's rest). Now arises the uneasy question: How can all this be accommodated in one day? When will I do this, when that? How shall I start on this and that? Thus agitated, we would like to run around and rush forth. We must then take the reins in hand and say, "Take it easy! Not any of this may touch me now. My first morning's hour belongs to the Lord. I will tackle the day's work which He charges me with, and He will give me the power to accomplish it."

So I will go to the altar of God. Here it is not a question of my minute, petty affairs, but of the great offering of reconciliation. I may participate in that, purify myself and be made happy, and lay myself with all my doings and troubles along with the sacrifice on the altar. And when the Lord comes to me then in Holy Communion, then I may ask Him, "Lord, what do you want of me?" (St. Teresa). And after quiet dialogue, I will go to that which I see as my next duty.

—*Saint Teresa Benedicta of the Cross (Edith Stein)*

64 | *The Paymaster*

His wage is everything you are and have in the natural order, for He bestows and preserves your being and life, and all the perfections of body and soul, as well as blessings that are eternal. His wage is also the spiritual gifts of His grace.... As though this wage were not enough, He has made Himself our wage, becoming a brother in our own flesh, as the price of our salvation on the cross and in the Eucharist to be with us as support and company. Oh, what an unworthy soldier he would be whom such a wage would not induce to labor for the honor of such a prince!... How extremely ungrateful and hard-hearted is he who after all this does not recognize his obligation to serve our Lord Jesus Christ diligently and to seek His honor!

—*Saint Ignatius of Loyola*

65 | *The Mass, Our Life*

The Mass is said in order that the whole Church and the whole of our life may become a mass, may become Christ's sacrifice always present on earth. St Francis de Sales resolved that he would spend the whole day preparing to say mass, so that whenever anyone asked him what he was doing, he might always answer, "I am preparing for Mass". We also could resolve to make our whole lives a participation in the divine mystery of the Redemption, so that when anyone puts the question to us, we can always answer, "I am saying Mass".

—*François Xavier Durrwell*

66 | *The Frenzy of Love*

Consider what is *most* beautiful and *most* noble on earth, what pleases the mind and the other faculties, and what delights the flesh and the senses. *Consider* the world, and the other worlds that shine in the night—the whole universe.

Well, this, along with all the satisfied follies of the heart, is worth nothing, *is* nothing and less than nothing, compared with this God of mine!—of yours! Infinite treasure, *most* beautiful pearl; humbled, become a slave, reduced to the form of a servant in the stable where he willed to be born, in Joseph's workshop, in his passion and in his ignominious death; and in the frenzy of Love—the blessed Eucharist.

—*Saint Josemaría Escrivá*

67 | *Place It on the Altar*

How often are you willing to inconvenience yourself or make a sacrifice for your neighbor, much less lay down your life for him? You are not always required to give your life for another, but you must always live for others. The true meaning of charity is more the giving of what you *are* than of what you *have*. Your neighbor does not require a portion of your money or possessions, but he longs for a portion of your heart. Love cannot exist unless it is based upon the gift of self that is self-sacrifice. St. Paul says, "Each one must do as he has made up his mind, not reluctantly or under compulsion, for God loves a cheerful giver" [2 Corinthians 9:7].

Because the sacrifice of Christ was so pleasing to God, He gladly accepts any offering or sacrifice on your part that you unite with it. Place upon the altar at Holy Mass the pains and sacrifices that human contacts demand of you, and make of them an expiatory offering in union with Christ. "As Christ loves us," you should be ready to sacrifice yourself for your neighbor, be it for the salvation of his soul or for the welfare of his temporal concern.

—*Lawrence G. Lovasik, S.V.D.*

68 | *The Imitation of the Eucharist*

In the Blessed Sacrament, Jesus is your model of a perfect life, your way to your home in Heaven. His presence among us teaches us many virtues that you must practice, the greatest of which is charity toward God and men. You can unite your acts of devotion with that perfect adoration, thanksgiving, atonement, and prayer that He offers to God without ceasing in the Holy Sacrament as an expression of His tender love for Him....

Here He leaves Himself entirely to the disposal of men. With what *patience* He bears with their coldness, irreverence, and negligence! He returns their ingratitude with kindly love.

With what perfect *obedience* He becomes present on our altars during holy Mass at the simple words of a priest!

You could not have a more beautiful model of *humility* than Jesus in the Blessed Sacrament. Glorious as is His risen Body, sublime as is His divinity, the eucharistic veil covers everything.... He is in truth a hidden God.

In the Blessed Sacrament, He exhorts you to *chastity*. By giving you His virginal Flesh in Holy Communion, He makes your body the temple and your soul the sanctuary of the infinitely holy God....

He teaches you *poverty*, for He is satisfied with the humble covering of the bread and wine, even lessening Himself within the limits of a tiny particle.

...Endeavor to imitate Him.

—*Lawrence G. Lovasik, S.V.D.*

69 | *The Sweet Life of God's Children*

Since we are the children of God, a chosen generation, a holy and kingly priesthood (1 Peter 2, 9), our aim and conduct in life should glow and shine with a courageous, active, patient love of sacrifice, until we have offered in the service of God and of the neighbor all our strength and goods, and the sacrifice of our own self shall be consummated. Such a life of sacrifice is, indeed, hard and painful to nature, but by the grace of God it becomes sweet and pleasing. The Sacrifice of Christ fortifies and strengthens unto patient endurance; from the altar peace and joy, comfort and refreshment daily flow to us.

—*Nicholas Gihr*

70 | *His Motives*

By creation He is our Father, by preservation our Sustainer and Guide, by justification our Redeemer. What is He by the Sacrament of the Altar? The relationship is so inexpressibly intimate as to be beyond our words. Now the motive which induced Him to do all this for us was not only sympathy, mercy and goodness, but boundless and self-forgetting love, which even now does not shrink from sacrifice. He could have made that sacrifice lighter; it would have sufficed if He had been present in one place in the world, if He had rejoiced us once in our lives by His visit to our souls and had made that visit only to those worthy of it. It would have sufficed if He were really present only at the moment of reception. He rejected all these limitations, and thus exposed Himself to a thousand indignities and irreverences. Let us not forget through what a bitter sea of ingratitude and injury He must pass every time He stands before our hearts that He may unite us sacramentally to Himself and knocks at the door like the Bridegroom in the Canticle of Canticles: "Open to me, My love, my head is full of dew, and My locks of the drops of the night." Where can we more fitly offer love for love to our Saviour than in the Most Holy Sacrament,...which is rightly called the Sacrament of Love? Although His perpetual Presence is with us everywhere and at every hour, yet in Holy Mass He offers Himself to us in the closest of all unions. How overwhelming a motive, how wonderful a means, for increasing continually in our love for Him!

—*Moritz Meschler, s.j.*

71 | *Applying His Merit*

You see, to hear Mass and/or to receive communion are spiritual *acts*. Not merely acts of worship but acts which have definite, specific merit. This merit can be applied to any other person either on earth or in purgatory. The merit of these acts does not, and this is crucial, proceed from the person performing the act. Since human merits, all of them in their entirety from the beginning of history, are not sufficient to compensate for the tiniest sin. For even the tiniest sin constitutes an act of spiritual rebellion against God. The tiniest imaginable sin is thus infinite in its enormity since it is a sin against an infinitely good, the only Absolute Being. Thus the merit, to return to the first point, of spiritual *acts* is derivative. It is derived from Christ. The infinite merit of His Incarnation, His infinitely humbling Himself, was alone sufficient to "liquidate" all human sins for all time. But the subsequent acts of His life have a mysterious value...which *naturally* (in their very nature) dwarf every historical event and every philosophical or scientific truth.

So in going to Mass and assisting at that bloodless sacrifice, one is simply applying the merits of Christ either to oneself or, as the phrase goes, to one's "friends and benefactors," known or unknown.

—Marshall McLuhan

72 | *What He Gives*

The Saviour and the Light
   Of all the human race
Gives, in this Holy Rite,
   A fount of endless grace.

Draw nigh, believing hearts,
   All pure and wholly shriven:
To you the Lord imparts
   Himself as pledge of heaven.

By whom all creatures live,
   The Lord of life and death,
Eternal life shall give
   To men of humble faith,

And shall their hunger quench
   With living, heavenly Bread,
Their thirsting spirit drench
   With living fountains fed.

—*Saint Sechnall*

73 | *The Perfect Sustenance*

When God desired to give a food to our soul to sustain
it in the pilgrimage of life, he looked upon creation and
found nothing that was worthy of it. Then he turned
again to himself, and resolved to give himself.

—*Saint John Vianney*

74 | *The Only Happiness*

Without the divine Eucharist there would be no happiness in this world; life would be unbearable. When we receive Holy Communion we receive our joy and happiness.

—*Saint John Vianney*

75 | *The Closest Union*

His union with those whom He loves surpasses every union of which one might conceive, and cannot be compared with any model.

Therefore even Scripture needed many illustrations to be able to express that connection, since one would not suffice. In one place it employs the figures of an inhabitant and a dwelling, in another those of a vine and a branch, here that of a marriage, there that of members and a head. None of those figures is adequate for that union, for it is impossible from these to attain to the exact truth. Above all it is necessary that the union should conform to friendship—yet what could be adequate for divine love?

…So I come to that which is strangest. To whom else could one be more closely united than to oneself? Yet this very unity is inferior to that union. For each of the spirits of the blessed ones is identical with himself, yet it is united to the Saviour more than to him. It loves the Saviour more than itself.

—*Nicholas Cabasilas*

76 | *Lose Yourself*

He who comes to Communion loses himself in God, as a drop of water in the ocean. They can be no more separated.

—*Saint John Vianney*

77 | *My Strength*

I find myself so weak that if it were not for Holy Communion I would fall continually. One thing alone sustains me, and that is Holy Communion. From it I draw my strength; in it is all my comfort. I fear life on those days when I do not receive Communion. I fear my own self. Jesus concealed in the Host is everything to me. From the tabernacle I draw strength, power, courage, and light. Here, I seek consolation in time of anguish. I would not know how to give glory to God if I did not have the Eucharist in my heart.

—*Saint Faustina Kowalska*

78 | *Growing in Grace*

Active union with Christ means an endeavor to practice, in one's conduct, the virtues of Christ. It means a constant effort to be pure like Him, to be spiritual like Him, to love God like Him, and to be kind and unselfish after His example. All Christ's acts sprang from, and were inspired by, grace. They had God as their ultimate objective, even though the immediate purpose was the alleviation of some human distress. If the Christian is to profit, as he ought, by the reception of the Blessed Sacrament he must strive after the ideal of Christian perfection. He must live habitually in a spirit of Faith and must aim at pleasing God, and not merely at not displeasing Him.... Life is dynamic. We cannot grow intimate with God by merely going mechanically and passively through a series of observances. This is the case even though these observances as instituted by Christ are, of themselves, sanctifying. If a man wishes his soul to grow in divine life through the reception of the Blessed Eucharist, he must supplement that reception, by the earnest endeavor to shape his conduct after the principles traced by Christ.... Active union with Christ means the effort to live like Christ. To hope for spiritual growth through the mere reception of the Eucharist, unaccompanied by any serious attempt to change one's character for the better, is to hope for the impossible.

—*Edward Leen, C.S.SP.*

79 | *The Pledge of Glory*

And just as a cutting from the vine planted in the ground bears fruit in its season, or as a grain of wheat falls into the earth and decomposes before rising with manifold increase,...so also our bodies, being nourished by [the Eucharist] and deposited in the earth, shall decompose there and rise at their appointed time, the Word of God granting them resurrection to the glory of God.

—*Saint Irenaeus of Lyons*

80 | *You Are Gods*

As the final end, the imparting of the sacrament comes:
transforming into itself those who receive it worthily, it
makes them, by grace and participation, similar to Him
who is good essentially, in no way inferior to Him, as far
as that is humanly possible and attainable for man.
Consequently, by adoption and grace, it is possible for
them to be and to be called gods, because all of God
completely fills them, leaving nothing in them empty of
His presence.

—*Saint Maximus the Confessor*

81 | *The Eucharistic Life*

The holiness of the Eucharist demands that those who
receive the sacrament do so with great reverence, lest
they defile what is holy. The church at all times bears in
mind the warning of Saint Paul, "Whoever eats of the
bread or drinks of the cup unworthily is guilty of pro-
faning the body and blood of the Lord" (1 Cor 11:27).
Conversely, those who become Christ's members by
feeding on his body take on new obligations. It would
be a profanation, Paul tells us, for them to enter into sex-
ual union with prostitutes (1 Cor 6:15–17). Pope John
Paul II in his encyclical reminds the faithful that they
should not receive Communion if they have committed
serious sin and have not been absolved in the sacrament
of Penance (*EE*, 36).

To be made holy by the Eucharist, it does not suffice
for us to be physically present at holy Mass or to receive
Communion physically. We must participate personally

by reverently hearing the Word of God and sharing in the mind of the church as she worships. The congregation is called to join in the church's self-offering, entering in spirit into Christ's own redemptive work (*Lumen Gentium*, No. 11).

Eucharistic holiness is never merely individual; it is ecclesial. The more closely the faithful are conjoined to Christ, the more intimately are they united to one another in his body. The attribute of holiness therefore leads directly into that of unity.

—*Cardinal Avery Dulles, S.J.*

82 | *Our Real Presence*

My first entrance into the Church of the Blessed Virgin Mary of Montenero, at Leghorn: At the elevation a young Englishman near me, forgetting decency, whispered, "This is their real presence." The shame I felt at his interruption, and the quick thought: If our Lord is not there, why did the Apostle threaten? How can he be blamed for not discerning the Lord's body if it is not there? How should they, for whom He has died, eat and drink their damnation (as says the Protestant text), if the Blessed Sacrament is but a piece of bread?

—*Saint Elizabeth Ann Seton*

83 | *The Word and the Flesh*

Heaven has *descended* into the world of matter; the supreme spiritual power is now operating by the machinery of matter, dealing miraculously with the bodies and souls of men. It blesses all the five senses; as the senses of the baby are blessed at a Catholic christening. It blesses even material gifts and keepsakes, as with relics or rosaries. It works through water or oil or bread or wine.... [T]he Incarnation is as much a part of that idea as the Mass; and...the Mass is as much a part of that idea as the Incarnation. A Puritan may think it blasphemous that God should become a wafer. A Moslem thinks it blasphemous that God should become a workman in Galilee.

—*G.K. Chesterton*

84 | *The Sense of It*

How I hate these follies of not believing in the Eucharist, etc.! If the Gospel be true, if Jesus Christ be God, what difficulty is there?

—*Blaise Pascal*

85 | *One on One*

[E]ach one alone with his Creator...who is reduced to the proportions of the most insignificant man and the poorest woman, to the degree of giving Himself to them as food if they want Him.... I feel a deep satisfaction ...in this absorption of the Creator by the creature. How many times since the twelfth of May 1896, when I made a good first communion, have I repeated and marveled at the words of Gounod's hymn sung on that morning: "Even to me You can descend, humility of my Savior!"

—*François Mauriac*

86 | *The Marvelous Exchange*

He who makes rich is made poor; he takes on the poverty of my flesh, that I may gain the riches of his divinity. He who is full is made empty; he is emptied for a brief space of his glory, that I may share in his fullness.

—*Saint Gregory Nazianzen*

87 | *Live and Rule in Me*

He belongs to you, but more than that, he longs to be in you, living and ruling in you, as the head lives and rules in the body. He desires that whatever is in him may live and rule in you: his breath in your breath, his heart in your heart, all the faculties of his soul in the faculties of your soul, so that these words may be fulfilled in you: *Glorify God and bear him in your body, that the life of Jesus may be made manifest in you.*

—*Saint John Eudes*

88 | *Nothing Better*

Nor can we do anything more pleasant. For what is better than God manifesting his whole sweetness to us.

—*Saint Albert the Great*

89 | *Martyr of the Eucharist*

On August 15, 255, a young man named Tarsicius, either an acolyte or a deacon of the Church of Rome, was walking the Appian Way, carrying a very special burden, the eucharistic Body of Christ. He moved carefully, to avoid dropping the Hosts in his possession, and it may have been the very care with which he moved that attracted attention. A group of nonbelievers confronted Tarsicius and demanded that he hand the Sacrament over to them. Tarsicius, fearing sacrilege, refused. The group then proceeded to attack Tarsicius with sticks and stones, beating him so violently that he died. But when the men searched Tarsicius' body, they found no trace of the Precious Body. After the mob, perhaps shaken by the miracle that had occurred in their midst or by their own casual brutality, dispersed, then the local Christians came and carried Tarsicius to the catacombs of Callistus for a Christian burial.

To this day, if you go into the catacombs of Callistus, you can read about the martyrdom of Tarsicius. Some one hundred years after the actual incident, Pope Damasus set up a memorial to this gruesome event, complete with a poem Damasus had composed himself: "While the holy Tarsicius was carrying the sacraments of Christ, an impious band pressed upon him, anxious to expose them to a profane gaze. He chose rather to give up his life than to betray the heavenly limbs to mad dogs."

—*Carl J. Sommer*

90 | *The Strangest Secret*

If God revealed himself to human beings continually, there would be no merit in believing him; and if he never revealed himself, there would be little faith indeed. But in fact he hides himself ordinarily and reveals himself only rarely to those who are anxious to do him service. This strange secret, in which God retires impenetrable to the sight of men, is a most important lesson to reflect upon in solitude. He remained hidden under the veil of nature with which we are enveloped until the incarnation. And even then he remained hidden in his humanity. He was much more recognizable when he was invisible than when he rendered himself visible. And finally when he wished to fulfill the promise made to his apostles—that he would stay with us all days, even to the consummation of the world—he chose to do so by abiding in the strangest and most obscure secret of all, in the species of the Eucharist. It is this sacrament that Saint John, in the Apocalypse, calls the "hidden manna" (Revelation 2:17); and I believe that Isaiah saw it in that state, when he said in the spirit of prophecy: "Truly you are a God who hides" (Isaiah 45:15). This is his ultimate secrecy. The veil of nature that covers God has been penetrated by some of the unbelieving, who, as Saint Paul says, have recognized an invisible God in visible nature. Heretical Christians have recognized him through his humanity and adored Jesus Christ God and man. But to recognize him under the species of bread is the privilege of Catholics alone; only to us has the hidden God revealed himself so fully.

—*Blaise Pascal*

91 | *Spiritual Communion*

[W]hen writing of the Prayer of Recollection, I spoke of the great importance of our entering into solitude with God. When you hear Mass without [receiving Communion], daughters, you may [make a spiritual communion], which is extremely profitable, and afterwards you may practise inward recollection in exactly the same way, for this impresses upon us a deep love of the Lord. If we prepare to receive Him, He never fails to give, and He gives in many ways that we cannot understand. It is as if we were to approach a fire: it might be a very large one, but, if we remained a long way from it and covered our hands, we should get little warmth from it, although we should be warmer than if we were in a place where there was no fire at all. But when we try to approach the Lord there is this difference: if the soul is properly disposed, and comes with the intention of driving out the cold, and stays for some time where it is, it will retain its warmth for several hours, *and if any little spark flies out, it will set it on fire.*

—*Saint Teresa of Avila*

92 | *Prayer Before Communion*

I wish, my Lord, to receive you with the purity, humility, and devotion with which your most holy Mother received you, with the spirit and fervor of the saints.

—*Traditional Prayer*

93 | *All of Him*

In the monastery of the Incarnation, and in the second year of my being prioress there, on the octave of St. Martin, when I was going to Communion, the Father, Fr. John of the Cross, divided the Host between me and another sister. I thought it was done, not because there was any want of Hosts, but that he wished to mortify me because I had told him how much I delighted in Hosts of a large size. Yet I was not ignorant that the size of the Host is of no moment; for I knew that our Lord is whole and entire in the smallest particle. His Majesty said to me: "Have no fear, My daughter; for no one will be able to separate thee from Me," giving me to understand that the size of the Host mattered not.

—Saint Teresa of Avila

94 | *Even the Least Particle*

The Body dispensed by the priest is as much in each particle as it is in the whole.... Each single recipient obtains nothing less than all [obtain] together: one has the whole, two have the whole, many receive the whole without diminution.

—Saint Caesarius of Arles

95 | *The Dignity of the Priest*

[I] desire to fear, love, and honor them [priests] and all others as my masters. And I do not wish to consider sin in them because I discern the Son of God in them and they are my masters. And I act in this way since I see nothing corporally of the Most High Son of God in this world except His Most Holy Body and Blood which they receive and which they alone administer to others. And these most holy mysteries I wish to have honored above all things and to be reverenced and to have them reserved in precious places.

—*Saint Francis of Assisi*

96 | *Speak With Him*

Do not go away directly after the holy Mass, but stay a moment to ask God to strengthen you well in your good resolutions.

—*Saint John Vianney*

97 | *The Best Prayer*

We need not speak so much to pray well. We know the good God is in the holy tabernacle. We open our hearts to him, and delight in his holy presence; that is the best prayer.

—*Saint John Vianney*

98 | *Gazing in Love*

[T]here was a man who never passed the church without entering it. In the morning when he went to work, and in the evening when he returned, he left his spade and his pickaxe at the door, and remained a long time in adoration before the Blessed Sacrament.... I asked him once what he said to our Lord during the long visits he paid him. Do you know what he answered? "Oh, I don't say anything to him, Monsieur le Curé, I *look at* him and he *looks at me.*"

—*Saint John Vianney*

99 | *Love Seeks Union*

A young wife, who had been taking instructions for a year, told the writer she could believe everything in the faith except the Eucharist. Upon inquiring about her husband, it was learned that he was in the Pacific on military duty. In answer to further questions, she admitted that she corresponded with him every two days and that she had his photograph before her in the house.

We argued there was nothing wanting for perfect happiness. What more could she want than the constant memory of him through the photograph and a written communication in which heart poured out to heart. But she protested that she could never be truly happy except through union with her husband.

But,...if human love craves oneness, shall not divine love? If husband and wife seek to be one in the flesh, shall not the Christian and Christ crave for that oneness with one another? The memory of the Christ who lived twenty centuries ago, the recalling of His mercy and miracles through memory, the correspondence with Him by reading the Scriptures—all these are satisfying, but they do not satisfy love. There must be, on the level of grace, something unitive with divine love. Every heart seeks a happiness outside it, and since perfect love is God, then the heart of man and the heart of Christ must, in some way, fuse. In human friendship the other person is loved as another self, or the other half of one's soul. Divine friendship must have its mutual "indwelling":

"He who dwells in love dwells in God and God in him" (I John 4:17). This aspiration of the soul for its ecstasy is fulfilled in the Sacrament of the Eucharist.

—Archbishop Fulton Sheen

100 | *How to Love*

Our Lord does not ask you to have two hearts, one for him and one for those you love here below.

Mothers, love our Eucharistic Lord with a mother's love. Love Him as your son. Wives, love Him as your husband. Children, love Him as your Father.

There is only one faculty of love in us....

—Saint Peter Julian Eymard

101 | *The Wait of Glory*

When you approach the tabernacle remember that *he* has been waiting for you for twenty centuries.

—Saint Josemaría Escrivá

102 | *Beloved*

It is pleasant to spend time with him, to lie close to his breast like the Beloved Disciple (cf. *Jn* 13:25) and to feel the infinite love present in his heart.

—Pope John Paul II

103 | *The Best Devotion*

Of all devotions, that of adoring Jesus in the Blessed Sacrament is the greatest after the sacraments, the one dearest to God and the one most helpful to us.

—*Saint Alphonsus Liguori*

104 | *What We Have*

In the Eucharist we have Jesus, we have his redemptive sacrifice, we have his resurrection, we have the gift of the Holy Spirit, we have adoration, obedience and love of the Father. Were we to disregard the Eucharist, how could we overcome our own deficiency?

—*Pope John Paul II*

105 | *The Eucharistic Throne*

"And I, if I be lifted up from the earth, will draw all things to myself."

It was from the height of His Cross that our Lord first drew all the souls to Himself by redeeming them. But when our Lord uttered these words, He certainly also had in mind His Eucharistic throne, to the foot of which He means to draw all souls so as to bind them there with the chains of His love.

—*Saint Peter Julian Eymard*

106 | *Making a Visit*

Education, government, instruction, and spiritual direction, how all these would be changed, how efficacious and liberating they would all become if parents, politicians, teachers and priests brought to their tasks the mysterious effacement of the Host, if their words became silent, and the exercise of their authority had no other purpose than to open the soul to the silence of God.

All speech and reasoning, all eloquence and science, all methods and all psychologies, all slogans and suggestions, are not worth a minute's silence, in which the soul, completely open, yields itself to the embrace of the Spirit.

This is the adorable secret of a visit to the Blessed Sacrament or a visit, possible even more frequently, to the Trinity present in our soul and in the souls of our brethren.

Is not this the first Church to build: the invisible cathedral erected in our hearts to the silent Word?

There is no theology more persuasive than this doctrine which cannot be reduced to formulas, taught by the invisible Doctor of Silence, whose lowered eyes spare our shame so lovingly, and whose generous Poverty clothes our wretchedness with such a redeeming compassion.

—*Maurice Zundel*

107 | *Resolutions*

"The heart in love goes with him, comes with him, stays with him always," Tasso said of the soul in love with God. That is what my life must be, centred in the Blessed Sacrament. I will never miss my daily visit and I will try to return to Jesus frequently during the rest of the day, if only to greet him. I must treat Jesus as I would treat a guest whom I am delighted to honor. My devotion to the Blessed Sacrament and the Sacred Heart must permeate my whole life, my thoughts and affections and all I do, so that I live only by it and with it. I must take great care over my preparation for Holy Mass and my thanksgiving afterwards.

—*Angelo Roncalli (later Pope John XXIII)*

108 | *My Wishes Before the Tabernacle*

O little key! I envy thee,
For thou canst ope, at any hour,
The Eucharistic prison-house,
Where dwells the God of Love and Power.
And yet—Oh, tender mystery!—
One effort of my faith alone
Unlocks the tabernacle door,
And hides me there with Christ my Own.

—*Saint Thérèse of Lisieux*

109 | *A Place to Rest*

I returned home light of heart,...begging our Lord to wrap my heart deep in that opened side,...or lock it up in His little tabernacle, where I shall now rest forever.

—*Saint Elizabeth Ann Seton*

110 | *Signs of Life*

If we loved our Lord, we should have that gilded tabernacle, that house of the good God, always before our mind's eye. When we see a spire from the road, that sight ought to make our hearts beat like the heart of a lover at sight of the roof under which his love dwells. We ought to be unable to take our eyes off it.

—*Saint John Vianney*

111 | *His Home*

Enthroned in His house is the Lord, awaiting us that we may enter and implore His mercy. It is not an ordinary dwelling, but a heaven upon earth, because the Lord of heaven resides therein.

—*Balaeus*

112 | *Sleepless*

[W]hen you awake in the night,...transport yourself quickly in spirit before the Tabernacle, saying: "Behold me, my God, I come to adore Thee, to praise, thank, and love Thee, and to keep Thee company with all the angels."

—*Saint John Vianney*

113 | *Moments That Matter*

The moments of our existence are not all the same....
But the point of points is the passage between this
short life and the other eternal one.

The Lord wants to be with us and to give us
courage at that moment. Here comes the priest into
our sickroom. He says, "Brother, receive the Viaticum
of the Body of our Lord Jesus Christ, may it defend
you from the evil enemy and lead you to eternal life!"
Those who know what the passage means, those who
believe in the very great love of Christ for us, are
happy to receive the Viaticum. A few days ago, when
Pope John [XXIII] learned from his doctor that he
was in grave danger, he immediately wanted the Lord.
And when the priest was in front of him, with the particle of the host raised, he paused first, made his pro-
fession of faith, asked forgiveness for his sins and for
the offenses he might possibly have given anyone, then
he received Communion. Still not content, he asked
that the Blessed Sacrament be exposed in his room,
and for a half hour, from his bed, he continued to contemplate and pray.

Here is the Eucharist! May it help us to die well
after it has helped us to live well. From our First
Communion to our Viaticum, may it influence our
life as Christians.

—*Albino Luciani (later Pope John Paul I)*

114 | *Iwo Jima, 1945*

The shell whizzed close, and both men ducked—the chaplain, Father Lawrence Lynch, and the battalion commander, Lieutenant Colonel Dennis Claire.

A sudden silence indicated the end of the salvo, and through it came a scream.

As the priest started forward, the commander grabbed his arm and told him not to be a fool.

"The boy is hurt...dying. I've got two minutes. I'll give him Communion and be back before the next salvo begins."

"You heard my orders. The litter bearers will bring him in. You belong in the aid station, where you can take care of all the casualties."

"You're wasting time, Denny. That's one of my boys. I can't let him die without the Blessed Sacrament." Father Lynch glanced at his watch. Time was running out.

As the colonel turned to his field phone to take a call, the chaplain scrambled to the nearby foxhole. Standing over the dying soldier, he lifted the Sacred Host: "*Corpus Domini nostri Jesu Christi custo...*"

The next salvo stopped him short. Shrapnel hit the chaplain's back and cut through his helmet, leaving a deep, ugly hole in his head.

The commander had heard the blast and dropped his phone. He ran to catch Father Lynch as he fell. Gently he pried open the dead chaplain's fingers and forced them to place the Viaticum on his own lips to prevent its desecration.

Oblivious to the shells, he lifted the chaplain's body and carried him back to base.

—*Adapted from* Father Cyclone, *by Daisy Amoury*

115 | *To Live for Him*

He makes it ever clearer to me that he wants me to burn with love for him in devotion to the Blessed Sacrament. Every time I receive him I must feel renewed that longing which stirs within me to live for Jesus only and to obtain the grace of preservation from so many sins which I should certainly commit if he did not come to my help. How can I remain deaf to his invitation?

—*Angelo Roncalli (later Pope John XXIII)*

116 | *Out of Darkness*

Out of the darkness of my life, so much frustrated, I put before you the one great thing to love on earth: the Blessed Sacrament.... There you will find romance, glory, honour, fidelity, and the true way of all your loves upon earth, and more than that: Death: by the divine paradox, that which ends life, and demands the surrender of all, and yet by the taste (or foretaste) of which alone can what you seek in your earthly relationships (love, faithfulness, joy) be maintained, or take on that complexion of reality, of eternal endurance, which every man's heart desires.

—*J.R.R. Tolkien*

117 | *Reflect the Glory*

You have learned these things, and been fully assured that what seems to be bread is not bread, though sensible to taste, but the Body of Christ. And what seems to be wine is not wine, though the taste will have it so, but the Blood of Christ. Long ago David sang of this, saying, "bread to strengthen man's heart, oil to make his face shine" (see Psalm 104:15). So strengthen your heart by spiritual partaking and make the face of your soul shine. Unveiled with a pure conscience, may you reflect as a mirror the glory of the Lord (see 2 Corinthians 3:18), and proceed from *glory to glory*, in Christ Jesus our Lord—to whom be honor, and might, and glory, for ever and ever. Amen.

—*Saint Cyril of Jerusalem*

118 | *There Is God*

Wherever the sacred Host is to be found, there is the living God, there is your Saviour, as really as when he was living and talking in Galilee and Judea, as really as he now is in heaven. Never deliberately miss Holy Communion. Communion is more than life, more than all the good things of this world, more than the whole universe: it is God himself, it is I, Jesus. Could you prefer anything to me? Could you, if you love me at all, however little, voluntarily lose the grace I give you in this way? Love me in all the breadth and simplicity of your heart.

—*Blessed Charles de Foucauld*

119 | *A* Magnificat

In the Eucharist the Church is completely united to Christ and his sacrifice, and makes her own the spirit of Mary. This truth can be understood more deeply by *re-reading the Magnificat* in a Eucharistic key. The Eucharist, like the Canticle of Mary, is first and foremost praise and thanksgiving. When Mary exclaims: "My soul magnifies the Lord and my spirit rejoices in God my Saviour," she already bears Jesus in her womb. She praises God "through" Jesus, but she also praises him "in" Jesus and "with" Jesus. This is itself the true "Eucharistic attitude".

At the same time Mary recalls the wonders worked by God in salvation history in fulfilment of the promise once made to the fathers (cf. *Lk* 1:55), and proclaims the wonder that surpasses them all, the redemptive incarnation. Lastly, the *Magnificat* reflects the eschatological tension of the Eucharist. Every time the Son of God comes again to us in the "poverty" of the sacramental signs of bread and wine, the seeds of that new history, wherein the mighty are "put down from their thrones" and "those of low degree are exalted" (cf. *Lk* 1:52), take root in the world. Mary sings of the "new heavens" and the "new earth" which find in the Eucharist their anticipation and in some sense their programme and plan. The *Magnificat* expresses Mary's spirituality, and there is nothing greater than this spirituality for helping us to experience the mystery of the Eucharist. The Eucharist has been given to us so that our life, like that of Mary, may become completely a *Magnificat!*

—*Pope John Paul II*

120 | *Power to Love*

Oh Mary, Mother of Jesus, give me your heart,
  so beautiful, so pure, so immaculate,
    so full of love and humility,
that I may be able to receive Jesus in the Bread of Life,
  love Him as you love Him, and serve Him
    in the distressing disguise
  of the Poorest of the Poor. Amen.

—*Blessed Mother Teresa of Calcutta*

The Voices

Saint Albert the Great (c. 1206–1280), a doctor of the Church, was a Dominican priest, noted theologian and teacher of Saint Thomas Aquinas.

Saint Ambrose (c. 337–397) was bishop of Milan. He is a father and doctor of the Church.

G.E.M. Anscombe (1919–2001) was a British analytic philosopher and convert to the Catholic faith.

Saint Thomas Aquinas (c. 1225–1274) was a Dominican priest and one of the greatest theologians of all time. He is called the Angelic Doctor. He composed the Office for the Solemnity of the Body and Blood of Christ.

April Oursler Armstrong (1926–2006), the daughter of famous Protestant evangelists, was a convert to Catholicism and apologist for the faith.

Saint Augustine of Hippo (354–430) is one of the most influential thinkers in world history. A bishop in North Africa, he was a prolific author and preacher.

Balaeus (d. 436) was a West Syrian bishop and poet.

The *Baltimore Catechism* was the United States Church's standard textbook for instruction in the Catholic faith from the late nineteenth through the mid-twentieth century.

Pope Benedict XVI (Joseph Ratzinger) (1927—) began his pontificate in 2005. He is a scholar of the liturgy and previously served as the Vatican's chief doctrinal official.

Nicholas Cabasilas (c. 1323–c. 1392) was a Greek monk, mystic and bishop.

Saint Caesarius of Arles (470–542), a father of the Church, was an influential bishop in Gaul (modern France).

Saint Catherine of Siena (1347–1380), a doctor of the Church, was a Dominican tertiary, a visionary and a reformer of the Church.

G.K. Chesterton (1874–1936) was an influential English man of letters and convert to Catholicism.

Saint Cyril of Jerusalem (313–386), a father and doctor of the Church, was a bishop renowned for the sacramental preparation he gave to adult converts to Christianity.

Dorothy Day (1897–1980), an American convert from atheism to Catholicism, was a founder of the Catholic Worker movement.

Avery Dulles (1918–2008) was an American theologian and Jesuit priest, named a cardinal by Pope John Paul II.

François Xavier Durrwell (1912–2005) was a French Redemptorist priest and renowned theologian.

Matthias Eberhard (1815–1876) was a German dogmatic theologian and bishop.

Ephrem of Syria (306–373), a doctor of the Church, was famed as a great teacher, orator, poet and defender of the faith.

Saint Josemaría Escrivá (1902–1975), a Spaniard, was the founder of Opus Dei, a way of holiness in ordinary work and family life.

Saint John Eudes (1601–1680) was a French missionary and the founder of two religious orders.

Saint Peter Julian Eymard (1811–1868) was a French Catholic priest and the founder of two religious orders.

Blessed Charles de Foucauld (1858–1916) lived as a hermit in the Sahara. He died as a martyr and inspired the founding of the Little Brothers of Jesus.

Saint Francis de Sales (1567–1622) was bishop of Geneva and a leader of the Catholic Reformation. He wrote the classic *Introduction to the Devout Life*.

Saint Francis of Assisi (1181–1226) was the founder of the Order of Friars Minor (the Franciscans). He bore the wounds of Christ on his body.

James Gibbons (1834–1921) was cardinal archbishop of Baltimore from 1877 until his death.

Nicholas Gihr (1839-1924), a German theologian, wrote a textbook on the Mass that was widely used in seminaries from the late nineteenth through the mid-twentieth century.

Romano Guardini (1885–1968) was an Italian-born priest and author who became one of the most important figures in Catholic intellectual life in twentieth-century Germany.

Scott Hahn (1957—) is an American biblical theologian and popular speaker and author. He founded the Saint Paul Center for Biblical Theology in Steubenville, Ohio.

Blessed Hildegard of Bingen (1098–1179) was a German abbess, visionary, composer and naturalist.

Conrad Hilton (1887–1979) was an American hotelier.

Saint Ignatius of Antioch (died c. 107), one of the apostolic fathers, was a bishop and martyr.

Saint Ignatius of Loyola (1491–1556) founded the Society of Jesus (the Jesuits).

Saint Irenaeus (c. 130–c. 202) was bishop of Lugdunum in Gaul (modern Lyons, France). He was a disciple of Saint Polycarp, who knew the apostle John. Irenaeus was a martyr and a father of the Church.

Saint James [Jacob] of Sarugh (451–521) was a monk, bishop, poet and theologian.

Blessed Pope John XXIII (1881–1963), baptized Angelo Roncalli, was the pontiff who summoned the Second Vatican Council. He reigned 1958–1963.

Saint John Chrysostom (c. 347–407) was bishop of Constantinople. A father of the Church, he is known as the Church's "Eucharistic Doctor."

Saint John of Damascus (676–749) was a Christian court official in the early Muslim caliphate. He entered monastic life and won renown as a theologian.

Pope John Paul I (1912–1978), baptized Albino Luciani, reigned as pontiff for only thirty-three days in 1978.

Pope John Paul II (1920–2005) reigned as pope for almost twenty-seven years (1978–2005), playing a key role in world events, such as the fall of communism. Before his pontificate he wrote profound poetry on the Eucharist, now published under his given name, Karol Wojtyla. He is popularly called "John Paul the Great."

Saint Justin Martyr (c. 100–c. 165) was a philosopher, a convert to the Christian faith from paganism and an apologist for Christian doctrine.

Saint Faustina Kowalska (1905–1938) was a Polish nun and mystic. From her visions of Jesus, she introduced the popular devotion to Divine Mercy.

Ronald Lawler (1926–2003) was a Capuchin priest, author, educator and member of the Pontifical Roman Theological Academy.

Edward Leen (1885–1944) was a Holy Ghost Father, renowned Irish educator, author and spiritual director.

Saint Alphonsus Liguori (1696–1787) was a bishop and founder of the Congregation of the Most Holy Redeemer (the Redemptorists).

The Liturgy of Saint James is a rite of the Eucharist used in the Eastern Churches. It dates back to the early centuries of Christianity.

Lawrence Lovasik, S.V.D., (1913–1986) was an American home missionary who served as pastor of immigrant parishes. He wrote many books in English and in Slovak.

The Martyrs of Abitina were forty-nine Christians found guilty, in 304, during the reign of the Emperor Diocletian, of illegally celebrating Sunday worship at Abitina, a town in the Roman province of Africa.

François Mauriac (1885–1970), a French novelist, won the Nobel Prize for Literature.

Saint Maximus the Confessor (c. 580–662) was a prominent imperial official before entering a monastery. Defending Catholic doctrine against a rising heresy, he incurred disfavor and was savagely tortured before his death.

Marshall McLuhan (1911–1980), media theorist, was among the most influential intellectuals of the twentieth century, coining phrases such as "global village" and "the medium is the message."

Moritz Meschler (1830–1912) was a Jesuit priest and influential spiritual writer.

Virgil Michel (1890–1938) was an American Benedictine monk and leader in the liturgical renewal.

Maria Montessori (1870–1952) was an Italian education reformer.

Saint Gregory Nazianzen (330–390), a father and doctor of the Church, is known as "The Theologian." He was a contemplative and a bishop.

Richard John Neuhaus (1936–2009), a former Lutheran pastor, was a convert to Catholicism and prominent American thinker on political and cultural matters.

Venerable John Henry Newman (1801–1890), a prolific English author, converted from Anglicanism to Roman Catholicism. An Oratorian priest, he was named a cardinal by Pope Leo XIII.

Blessed Frederic Ozanam (1813–1853), a French scholar, was founder of the Society of Saint Vincent de Paul.

Blaise Pascal (1623–1662), a devout French layman, was an influential mathematician and physicist. He made important contributions to the development of computing machines.

Saint Pio of Pietrelcina (1887–1968) was a Capuchin priest and mystic who bore the wounds of Christ in his body.

Saint Pius X (1835–1914), pope from 1903 to 1914, was a catalyst in the liturgical renewal, promoting frequent Communion and lowering the age of First Communion.

Aymon-Marie Roguet (1906–1991) was a French Dominican priest and liturgical scholar.

Saint Sechnall (c. 372–457) was, according to Irish tradition, a nephew of Saint Patrick who helped bring the faith to Ireland.

The Second Vatican Council (1962-1965) was the twenty-first ecumenical council of the Church.

Saint Elizabeth Ann Seton (1774–1821) was the first native-born citizen of the United States to be canonized. She was a wife, mother and foundress of a religious order.

Fulton J. Sheen (1895–1979) was an archbishop who hosted top-rated television and radio shows. He was a tireless promoter of Catholic foreign missions.

Carl J. Sommer (1961—) is a husband, father and independent scholar of early Christianity.

Saint Bernadette Soubirous (1844–1879) had visions of the Blessed Virgin Mary at Lourdes in France. She later became a Sister of Charity.

Robert Spitzer (1952—) is a Jesuit priest, scholar, author and educator.

Carroll Stuhlmueller (1923–1994) was a Passionist priest and noted American biblical scholar.

Saint Teresa of Avila (1515–1582), a doctor of the Church, was a Spanish mystic and great reformer of the Carmelite order.

Saint Teresa Benedicta of the Cross (Edith Stein, 1891–1942) was a German philosopher who converted from Judaism to Catholicism, entered a Carmelite monastery and died a martyr at Auschwitz.

Blessed Mother Teresa of Calcutta (1910–1997) was an Albanian nun who founded the Missionaries of Charity and served almost half a century in the slums of Calcutta, India. She was awarded the Nobel Peace Prize.

Saint Thérèse of Lisieux (1873–1897), known as the "Little Flower," was a French Carmelite nun whose memoirs, published after her death, gained many devotees to her spiritual path, her "Little Way." She is a doctor of the Church.

Thomas à Kempis (c. 1380–1471) was a German monk and author of *The Imitation of Christ*.

J.R.R. Tolkien (1892–1973) was an English novelist and scholar, best known for his *Lord of the Rings* trilogy.

Saint John Vianney (1786–1859) served as a humble curate in rural French parishes. He is patron saint of parish priests.

Saint Vladimir of Kiev (956–1015) converted to Christianity, with his people, in 987 after sending emissaries abroad to enquire about the major religions.

George Weigel (1951—) is a prominent American biographer and commentator.

Maurice Zundel (1897–1975) was a Swiss priest, philosopher and liturgist.

Sources

Introduction

1. *Didascalia Apostolorum*, quoted in Lucien Deiss, C.S.SP., *Springtime of the Liturgy: Liturgical Texts of the First Four Centuries*, Matthew J. O'Connell, trans. (Collegeville, Minn.: Liturgical, 1979), p. 174.

2. John Chrysostom, *Homilies on the Gospel of Matthew*, Homily 50, nos. 3–4: *PG* 58, pp. 508–509, as quoted in John Paul II, *Dies Domini*, Apostolic Letter on Keeping the Lord's Day Holy, July 5, 1998, available at: www.vatican.va.

Quotes

1. Pope Saint Pius X, address to the Confraternity of the Blessed Sacrament, quoted in Joseph A. Dunney, *The Mass* (New York: MacMillan, 1948), p. 308, and available at: www.fatima.org.

2. Sermon of John Vianney, as quoted in Abbé H. Convert, ed., *Eucharistic Meditations: Extracts From the Writings and Instructions of Saint John Vianney*, Mary Benvenuta, O.P., trans. (Trabuco Canyon, Calif.: Source, 1993), p. 89.

3. Patricia McEachern, ed., *A Holy Life: The Writings of Saint Bernadette of Lourdes* (San Francisco: Ignatius, 2005), pp. 130–131.

4. Maria Montessori, *The Mass: Explained to Children* (Fort Collins, Col.: Roman Catholic Books, 1932), pp. 8–9.

5. Humphrey Carpenter, ed., *The Letters of J.R.R. Tolkien* (Boston: Houghton Mifflin, 1981), pp. 338–339.

6. Robert Spitzer, *Five Pillars of the Spiritual Life: A Practical Guide to Prayer for Active People* (San Francisco: Ignatius, 2008), p. 17.

7. Sermon of John Vianney, as quoted in Convert, pp. 147–148.

8. Frederic Ozanam, as quoted in Leo Knowles, *Catholic Book of Quotations* (Huntington, Ind.: Our Sunday Visitor, 2004), p. 246.

9. Quoted in Eileen Dunn Bertanzetti, ed., *Padre Pio's Words of Hope* (Huntington, Ind.: Our Sunday Visitor, 1999), p. 82.

10. Adapted from Ambrose of Milan, *On the Sacraments* 5.4, in Scott Hahn and Mike Aquilina, *Living the Mysteries: A Guide for Unfinished Christians* (Huntington, Ind.: Our Sunday Visitor, 2003), pp. 161–162.

11. Conrad N. Hilton, *Be My Guest* (New York: Fireside, 1994), p. 150.

12. Maurice Zundel, *The Splendour of the Liturgy* (New York: Sheed & Ward, 1944), p. 169.

13. Richard John Neuhaus, *Catholic Matters: Confusion, Controversy, and the Splendor of Truth* (New York: Basic, 2006), pp. 115–116.

14. Ronald Lawler, O.F.M. CAP. "Ordinary Faith in the Eucharist," in *Catholic Dossier*, September–October 1996, p. 29.

15. George Weigel, *Letters to a Young Catholic* (New York: Basic, 2004), p. 147.

16. Nicholas Gihr, *The Holy Sacrifice of the Mass: Dogmatically, Liturgically and Ascetically Explained* (St. Louis: Herder, 1929), p. 198.

17. Quoted in Geoffrey Wainwright and Karen B. Westerfield Tucker, eds., *The Oxford History of Christian Worship* (New York: Oxford University Press, 2006), p. 266.

18. Josemaría Escrivá, *The Way*, no. 529 (Manila: Sinag-tala, 1982), p. 177.

19. Thomas à Kempis, *The Imitation of Christ* (Milwaukee: Bruce, 1949), bk. 4, chap. 2, no. 6, available at: www.ccel.org.

20. Blessed Hildegard of Bingen, *Scivias* 2.6.10, quoted in Wainwright and Tucker, p. 206.

21. John Chrysostom, as quoted in Jean Danielou, *The Angels and Their Mission*, David Heimann, trans., (Notre Dame, Ind.: Christian Classics, 1994), pp. 66–67.

22. Josemaría Escrivá, *Holy Rosary* (New York: Scepter, 2003), appendix.

23. See Massey H. Shepherd, Jr., *The Worship of the Church*, vol. 4 (Greenwich, Conn.: Seabury, 1852), pp. 3–4.

24. A.-M. Roguet, O.P., *Holy Mass: Approaches to the Mystery* (Collegeville, Minn.: Liturgical, 1960), p. 84.

25. Ignatius of Antioch, *To the Romans*, chaps. 4, 7, adapted from Roberts, et al., eds., *Ante-Nicene Fathers*, (Buffalo, N.Y.: Christian Literature, 1885) vol. 1, pp. 75–77, available at: www.newadvent.org.

26. S.L. Emery, trans., *Poems of St. Teresa, Carmelite of Lisieux, Known as the "Little Flower of Jesus"* (Boston: Angel Guardian, 1907), available at: www.ccel.org.

27. Pope John XXIII, *Journal of a Soul*, Dorothy White, trans. (New York: Signet, 1965), p. 215.

28. Justin Martyr, *Dialogue With Trypho*, chap. 41, adapted from Roberts, available at: www.newadvent.org.

29. Ephrem of Syria, *Hymns on the Nativity*, Hymn 3, adapted from J.B. Morris, trans., Philip Schaff, ed., *Nicene and Post-Nicene Fathers, Second Series* vol. 13, available at: www.newadvent.org.

30. Third Plenary Council of Baltimore, *A Catetchism of Christian Doctrine*, supplemented by Thomas L. Kinkead (New York: Benziger, 1921), pp. 185–186.

31. Blessed Hildegard of Bingen, *Scivias* 2.6.14, quoted in Wainwright and Tucker, p. 206.

32. François Xavier Durrwell, in Martin Redfern, ed., *Theologians Today: F.X. Durrwell, C.SS.R.* (New York: Sheed and Ward, 1972), pp. 89–90.

33. Excerpt from Thomas Aquinas, *Pange Lingua,* Edward Caswall, trans., available at: www.preces-latinae.org.

34. G.E.M. Anscombe, "On Transubstantiation," excerpted from *The Collected Philosophical Papers of G.E.M. Anscombe*, vol. 3 (Oxford: Blackwell, 1981), pp. 107–112, available at: www.secondspring.co.uk.

35. Quoted in David Scott, ed., *Praying in the Presence of Our Lord With Dorothy Day* (Huntington, Ind.: Our Sunday Visitor, 2002), pp. 100–101.

36. Romano Guardini, *Meditations Before Mass* (Manchester, N.H.: Sophia Institute, 1993), p. 146.

37. April Oursler Armstrong, *House With a Hundred Gates* (New York: McGraw-Hill, 1965), p. 156.

38. Adapted from John of Damascus, *An Exposition of the Orthodox Faith*, bk. 4, ch. 13, in Morris and Schaff, vol. 9, p. 82, available at: www.newadvent.org.

39. Adapted from Saint John Chrysostom, *Homilies on First Corinthians*, Homily 24, nos. 3, 4, 8, in Philip Schaff, ed., *Nicene and Post-Nicene Fathers, First Series*, vol. 12 (Buffalo, N.Y.: Christian Literature, 1889), available at: www.newadvent.org.

40. Ambrose of Milan, *On the Sacraments* 4.4.14–16, in *St. Ambrose "'On the Mysteries' and the Treatise 'On the Sacraments,'"* T. Thompson, B.D., trans. (London: SPCK, 1919), pp. 109–111.

41. Saint Justin Martyr, *Apology* 1.65–67, quoted in *Catechism of the Catholic Church*, (Washington, D.C.: USCCB, 1997) #1345.

42. Homily of St. James of Sarugh used in the *Liturgy of St. James*, quoted in Wainwright and Tucker, p. 159.

43. Ephrem of Syria, adapted from a hymn translated in E.B. Pusey, *The Doctrine of the Real Presence* (London: John Henry Parker, 1855), p. 122.

44. John Chrysostom, *Homilies on Matthew*, Homily 82, n. 5, adapted from Schaff, vol. 10, p. 495, available at: www.newadvent.org.

45. Jean-François Six, ed., *Spiritual Autobiography of Charles de Foucauld* (Denville, N.J.: Dimension, 1964), p. 98.

46. *Coptic Anaphora of Saint Basil*, quoted in Wainwright and Tucker, p. 138.

47. Venerable John Henry Newman, *Discourses to Mixed Congregations* (London: Longmans, Green, 1906), pp. 267–268, available at: www.newmanreader.org.

48. John Vianney, as quoted in Convert, p. 20.

49. Augustine, *Sermons*, 272, author's translation.

50. Francis de Sales, *Introduction to the Devout Life*, part 2, ch. 2, adapted from the edition available at: www.ccel.org.

51. Catherine of Siena, as quoted in Benedict Groeschel, *Praying In The Presence Of Our Lord: Prayers for Eucharistic Adoration* (Huntington, Ind.: Our Sunday Visitor, 1998), p. 44.

52. James Gibbons, *The Faith of Our Fathers* (Baltimore: John Murphy, 1892), p. 362.

53. *Liturgy of St. James*, quoted in Wainwright and Tucker, p. 159.

54. Carroll Stuhlmueller, C.P., *Thirsting for the Lord* (Garden City, N.Y.: Image, 1979), pp. 159–160.

55. John Chrysostom, *On the Priesthood*, bk. 3, no. 4, adapted from Schaff, vol. 9, p. 46, available at: www.ccel.org.

56. Quoted in Bertanzetti, p. 82.

57. Second Vatican Council, *Dogmatic Constitution on the Church: Lumen Gentium*, no. 34, available at: www.ewtn.com.

58. Matthias Eberhard, quoted in Gihr, p. 214.

59. Quoted in Robert L. Tuzik, ed., *How Firm a Foundation: Leaders of the Liturgical Movement* (Chicago: Liturgy Training Publications, 1990), p. 154.

60. Scott Hahn, *The Lamb's Supper: The Mass as Heaven on Earth* (New York: Doubleday, 1999), pp. 162–163.

61. Pope Benedict XVI, Post-Synodal Apostolic Exhortation *Sacramentum Caritatis*, no. 86, available at: www.vatican.va.

62. Pope Benedict XVI, Address Welcoming Young People to World Youth Day, Cologne, Germany, August 18, 2005, available at: www.vatican.va.

63. Edith Stein, *Essays on Woman* (Washington, D.C.: ICS, 1987), pp. 130–131.

64. William J. Young, S.J., ed., *Letters of St. Ignatius of Loyola* (Chicago: Loyola University Press, 1959), pp. 124–125.

65. Redfern, pp. 97–98.

66. Quoted in Andrés Vázquez de Prada, *The Founder of Opus Dei: The Life of Josemaría Escrivá,* vol. 3 (Princeton, N.J.: Scepter, 2005), vol. 3, p. 288.

67. Lawrence G. Lovasik, *The Hidden Power of Kindness* (Manchester, N.H.: Sophia Institute, 1999), p. 32.

68. Lawrence G. Lovasik, *The Basic Book of the Eucharist* (Manchester, NH: Sophia Institute, 2001), pp. 30–31.

69. Gihr, p. 226.

70. Moritz Meschler, S.J., *Three Fundamental Principles of the Spiritual Life* (St. Louis: Herder, 1912), pp. 230–231.

71. Marshall McLuhan, "Spiritual Acts: Letter to Corinne Lewis," in *The Medium and the Light: Reflections on Religion* (Toronto: Stoddart, 1999), pp. 24–25.

72. From the Latin hymn *Sancti Venite*, in Hugh T. Henry, L.H.D., *Eucharistica: Verse and Prose in Honour of the Hidden God* (Philadelphia: Dolphin, 1912), p. 79.

73. John Vianney, *Esprit*, pp. 140–141, as quoted in Convert, p. 44.

74. Sermon of John Vianney, as quoted in Convert, p. 79.

75. Nicholas Cabasilas, *The Life in Christ* (Crestwood, N.Y.: St. Vladimir's Seminary Press, 1974), p. 46.

76. John Vianney, as quoted in Convert, p. 58.

77. George Kosicki, *Revelations of Divine Mercy: Daily Readings from the Diary of Blessed Faustina Kowalska* (Ann Arbor, Mich.: Servant, 1996), p. 282.

78. Edward Leen, *The True Vine and Its Branches* (New York: P.J. Kenedy, 1938), pp. 96–97.

79. Irenaeus, *Against Heresies*, bk. 5, ch. 2, no. 3, adapted from Roberts, vol. 1, p. 528, available at: www.ccel.org.

80. Julian Stead, trans., *The Church, the Liturgy and the Soul of Man: The Mystagogia of St. Maximus the Confessor* (Still River, Mass.: St. Bede's, 1982), p. 96.

81. Avery Dulles, "A Eucharistic Church," *America Magazine*, December 20, 2004, available at: www.americamagazine.org.

82. Quoted in Madame De Barberey, *Elizabeth Seton* (Emmitsburg, Md.: Mother Seton Guild Press, 1957), pp. 354–355.

83. G.K. Chesterton, *The Thing: Why I Am a Catholic* (London: Sheed and Ward, 1929), available at: www.cse.dmu.ac.uk.

84. Blaise Pascal, *Pascal's Pensées* (New York: E.P. Dutton, 1958), p. 63.

85. François Mauriac, *What I Believe*, Wallace Fowlie, trans. (New York: Farrar, Straus, 1963), pp. 20–21.

86. Gregory Nazianzen, excerpt from *Oratio* 45, Divine Office for Tuesday of first week in Advent.

87. John Eudes, excerpt from a treatise on the admirable Heart of Jesus, Divine Office for August 19.

88. Albert the Great, from *Commentary on the Gospel of Luke,* Divine Office for November 15.

89. Carl J. Sommer, *We Look for a Kingdom: The Everyday Lives of the Early Christians* (San Francisco: Ignatius, 2007), p. 134.

90. Blaise Pascal, "Letter to Mlle. de Roannez," October 1656, in *Œuvres Complètes de Blaise Pascal* (Paris: Edition de Ch. Lahure, 1858), author's translation.

91. Teresa of Avila, *The Way of Perfection* (New York: Doubleday Image, 1968), ch. 35, available at: www.ccel.org.

92. James Socias, ed., *Handbook of Prayers* (Woodridge, Ill.: Midwest Theological Forum, 2007), p. 322.

93. Teresa of Avila, "Relations" (or "Spiritual Testimonies"), Relation 3, no. 19, in *The Life of St. Teresa of Jesus, of The Order of Our Lady of Carmel* (New York: Benziger, 1904), available at: www.ccel.org.

94. Caesarius of Arles, quoted in Joseph Pohle, *The Sacraments: A Dogmatic Treatise*, Arthur Preuss, ed. (St. Louis: Herder, 1919), vol. 2, p. 97.

95. Francis of Assisi, "Testament," quoted in Wainwright and Tucker, p. 236

96. John Vianney, quoted in Convert, p. 103.

97. John Vianney, quoted in Convert, pp. 117–118.

98. John Vianney, quoted in Convert, p. 118.

99. Fulton J. Sheen, *These Are the Sacraments* (New York: Hawthorn, 1962), p. 49.

100. Peter Julian Eymard, "Let Us Love the Most Blessed Sacrament," available at: www.ewtn.com.

101. Escrivá, *The Way*, no. 537, p. 147.

102. Pope John Paul II, encyclical letter *Ecclesia de Eucharistia*, no. 25, available at: www.vatican.va.

103. Alphonsus Liguori, as quoted in Pope John Paul II, *Ecclesia de Eucharistia*, no. 25.

104. Pope John Paul II, *Ecclesia de Eucharistia*, no. 60.

105. Peter Julian Eymard, "Let Us Love the Most Blessed Sacrament."

106. Zundel, pp. 127–128.

107. Pope John XXIII, p. 236.

108. Thérèse of Lisieux, "My Wishes Before the Tabernacle," in *Poems of St. Teresa, Carmelite of Lisieux, Known as the "Little Flower of Jesus"* (Boston: Angel Guardian, 1907), available at: www.ccel.org.

109. Quoted in Mary Coyle O'Neil, *Mother Elizabeth Ann Seton* (Emmitsburg, Md.: Mother Seton Guild, 1940), p. 34.

110. John Vianney, quoted in Convert, p. 41.

111. Quoted in Gihr, p. 104.

112. Quoted in Joseph Vianney, *The Blessed John Vianney: Curé d'Ars, Patron of Parish Priests* (London: Duckworth, 1906), p. 185.

113. Homily for Corpus Christi 1963, quoted in Raymond and Lauretta Seabeck, *The Smiling Pope: The Life and Teaching of John Paul I* (Huntington, Ind.: Our Sunday Visitor, 2004), pp. 141–142.

114. Adapted from Daisy Amoury, *Father Cyclone: The True Story of a Remarkable Catholic Chaplain Who Served in the Pacific* (New York: Julian Messner, 1958), pp. 251–253.

115. Pope John XXIII, p. 200.

116. Carpenter, pp. 53–54.

117. Cyril of Jerusalem, Mystagogical Lecture 4, no. 9, adapted from Morris and Schaff, vol. 7, p. 152, available at: www.ccel.org.

118. Six, p. 99.

119. Pope John Paul II, *Ecclesia de Eucharistia*, no. 58.

120. Quoted in Susan Conroy, *Mother Teresa's Lessons of Love and Secrets of Sanctity* (Huntington, Ind.: Our Sunday Visitor, 2003), p. 116.

Angels of God
The Bible, the Church and the Heavenly Hosts

• • •

Drawing on Scripture (where angels appear often, carrying out crucial tasks), the words of the saints and Church teaching, Mike Aquilina shows how developing our "fellowship with the angels is not an ornament on our religion, it's a life skill."

Order #T16898
ISBN 978-0-86716-898-3
$12.99

Love in the Little Things
Tales of Family Life
FOREWORD BY SCOTT HAHN

• • •

Love involves sacrifice, Mike Aquilina notes, but as he spins humorous stories from his own family, it is evident that moms, dads and kids are happier when they lay down their lives for one another. *Love in the Little Things* nudges the reader toward a more satisfying family life.

Order #T16814
ISBN 978-0-86716-814-3
$12.99

GINA LOEHR

Choosing Beauty
A 30-Day Spiritual Makeover
for Women

• • •

Mascara will help and eyeliner too,
but the surest way to a beautiful you
doesn't require hours at the cosmetics
counter. The best beauty routine starts
within. *Choosing Beauty* guides you
through a day-by-day inner makeover
that will give you a glow that can only
come through a life infused with the
virtues. Learn how to step away from
gossip, grow in courage, practice
mercy and enter more fully into the
qualities that will allow your inner light
to shine. Suitable for individual use or
group study.

Order #T16921
ISBN 978-0-86716-921-8
$12.99

FATHER DAVE PIVONKA,
T.O.R.

Hiking the Camino
500 Miles With Jesus

• • •

You might reasonably wonder why anyone would shoulder a heavy backpack, grab a walking stick and hike across Spain. Whatever happened to planes, trains and automobiles? But Father Dave Pivonka knew that the Camino—the ancient pilgrim path to the tomb of Saint James the Apostle in Santiago—offered an opportunity to focus on God in the stripped-down environment typical of the religious journey known as a pilgrimage.

Father Dave takes you along with him, eager to show that God wants to take care of you whether or not you can see down the road or, if tired and sore, you're tempted to quit. His Camino hike holds real lessons for your own life's journey.

Order #T16882
ISBN 978-0-86716-882-2
$13.99